Advance Praise
for *Faith, Hope & Politics*

Is there a way forward in our political climate that can re-stitch the fraying social fabric and deliver a more durable and beautiful tapestry of public life together? Brent McDougal is a student and practitioner of politics and religion, as well as the virtues that underlie them. He proposes the contours of character that will knit us back together, inside and out.

—George A. Mason
Senior Pastor, Wilshire Baptist Church
Dallas, Texas

I have known Dr. Brent McDougal to be a true servant leader in his church and his community. He has penned a most fascinating book with a call to action that will challenge all Christian believers to be the salt and light in our country.

—Gary Cook
Chancellor, Dallas Baptist University

I am convinced that more people today are called to politics than are answering the call. Dr. McDougal has delivered a penetrating work that peers into the soul with conviction and a call to action. This deeply insightful and practical book is a must read!

—Adam C. Wright
President, Dallas Baptist University

Brent McDougal lays out a compelling case for millennials to become more politically active. *Faith, Hope & Politics* illustrates the principles one employs to turn their faith into works in our democracy. I highly recommend the book and its author.

—Judge Clay Lewis Jenkins
Dallas County, Texas

Smyth & Helwys Publishing, Inc.
6316 Peake Road
Macon, Georgia 31210-3960
1-800-747-3016
©2018 by Brent McDougal
All rights reserved.

Library of Congress Cataloging-in-Publication Data

Names: McDougal, Brent P., 1970- author.
Title: Faith, hope & politics : inspiring a new generation to
community-changing political engagement / by Brent McDougal.
Description: Macon : Smyth & Helwys, 2018.
Identifiers: LCCN 2017051051 | ISBN 9781573129923 (pbk. : alk. paper)
Subjects: LCSH: Generation Y--Religious life. | Generation Y--Conduct of
life. | Generation Y--Political activity.
Classification: LCC BV4529.2 .M378 2017 | DDC 261.70973--dc23
LC record available at https://lccn.loc.gov/2017051051

FAITH, HOPE & POLITICS

Inspiring a New Generation to **Community-Changing** Political Engagement

BRENT MCDOUGAL

Also by Brent McDougal

The River of the Soul: A Spirituality Guide for Christian Youth

For Jen, my best friend

Nothing that is worth doing can be achieved in our lifetime; therefore we must be saved by hope. Nothing which is true or beautiful or good makes complete sense in any immediate context of history; therefore we must be saved by faith. Nothing we do, however virtuous, can be accomplished alone; therefore we must be saved by love. No virtuous act is quite as virtuous from the standpoint of our friend or foe as it is from our standpoint. Therefore we must be saved by the final form of love which is forgiveness.

—Reinhold Niebuhr

If we could change ourselves, the tendencies in the world would also change. As a man changes his own nature, so does the attitude of the world change towards him. . . . We need not wait to see what others do.

—Mahatmas Gandhi

Contents

Introduction

As a freshman in college, I was eager to become more "political." I grew up around lawmakers and lobbyists in the Alabama legislature, and as an eighteen-year-old idealist I was ready to make a difference. This led me to run for student government, attend political functions in Georgia (I earned my undergraduate degree at Emory University in Atlanta), pursue leadership in my fraternity, engage in endless debates, and participate in rallies and protests for positive change.

One particular protest would change my life.

The Ku Klux Klan marched in downtown Atlanta in January 1989 to oppose the Martin Luther King Jr. holiday. Perhaps their biggest motivation was to remind the public that they were still alive, resistant to change, and angry as ever.

My roommate and I took our place against the guardrails near the federal courthouse to protest the KKK's message of racism and division, and I can still feel the tension in the crowd and the sense that violence lurked just under the surface. I held up a homemade sign that read "No More Hate" as we waited for the march to wind towards us.

A surreal scene began to unfold as we watched the marchers make their way down a long street in our direction. Only seven white supremacists walked in their demonstration, but more than 2,000 National Guardsmen, Georgia Bureau of Investigation agents, and prison guards had been deployed. Sharpshooters dotted the rooftops and lines of armed police officers extended everywhere. I could barely make out the marchers, who were completely surrounded—perhaps fifteen deep on each side—by their protectors.

The marchers carried their own sign that said "No King Over Us." As they approached our spot, the crowd began to shout, jostle around, and wave their fists. Then a brick flew over my head towards the marchers, and everything changed.

Suddenly we were in the middle of a riot.

Rocks flew in every direction. People screamed. The crowd completely dissolved in a panic. I felt very afraid and uncertain what to do, wanting nothing more than to get away. Whenever my roommate and I started to run in one direction, we were met by police in riot gear and forced to go in another. I was pushed down by an officer with a shield, and this was confusing. I wasn't threatening or in any way displaying violence. My roommate seemed to be enjoying himself in the chaos, but I felt frightened and powerless.

We finally found a long route back to the car and returned safely to campus. Turning on the news, we could hardly believe that we were in the middle of what was being reported: cars on fire, tear gas clouding the streets, people running in every direction. I listened to angry interviews of the protesters.

It dawned on me that those who were protesting hatred and violence seemed to mirror the same hatred and violence. Nothing about that day brought anyone closer together. Freedom of expression, one of our most cherished values, was represented in both the march and the protest. But something broke down in the way it was exercised.

For me, that protest and riot were a kind of wake-up call to the harsh realities of the world and also to the courage and commitment it would take to make the world a better place. I arrived with a sense of power (the power of protest, the power of positive change), but I left in fear. Those who were marching likely felt more justified in their hatred, and those who rioted returned hate for hate.

Most of us just felt stuck in the middle.

Like many people younger than I am, I've had great visions of wanting to change the world. I still believe that I can make a difference, even in mid-career. In fact, I believe it now more than ever. But I have also experienced what it feels like to be "stuck"—caught between a vision of beauty and a fear of what can happen when you start to speak up and be the change you want to see. I know the feeling of powerlessness.

So many young people today lack the belief that things can and will get better. On the one hand, there's great hopefulness for a better world. On the other hand, there's little confidence that life as we know it will get anything but worse. They see the politics of division, name-calling, and ridiculous grandstanding. They see an economy that mostly benefits the rich and edges out the poor. They have little trust in political solutions to our biggest problems.

In today's political climate, people often feel pessimistic and resigned. Power always seems to be in the hands of someone else. Why try when those in power always seem to find a way to stay in power? Many young people have rejected politics as no more than self-interested, money-driven, ego-infested posturing that lacks practical application. George Bernard Shaw said, "He knows nothing; and he thinks he knows everything. That points clearly to a political career."[1] This caricature drives young people to pursue careers in business, nonprofit work, or education in order to change the world, but what about politics and public service? No thanks.

That's why I'm writing this book. It's a call to action with underlying principles and inspiration to encourage young people not only to *hear* the call to public service but also to *respond.*

I'm writing because young people often feel they don't have any power, but that is simply not true. Those with faith, hope, and love always have more power than they can imagine.

I'm writing this book because, now more than ever, we need young people with courage and compassion to develop a practice of politics different from the brand of my generation.

I'm writing because people have manipulated and abused the political process such that we all become complicit, disgruntled, and cynical. A select few have taken the arena where we work out our highest ideals of society and co-opted them for either personal power or a tribal victory.

I'm writing because I am afraid that people's distrust of politics and government will lead to a distrust and rejection of democracy, which would be a disaster for America.

I'm writing because I believe that there are many people who want to act out of their faith identity, however that may be expressed, but don't feel like politics is a good arena in which to be who they are.

I want to call young people of goodwill to take up the challenge of sacrifice and service in an area many have abandoned. I'm writing this book because I want to inspire the next generation to see the good that can come from politics and government service.

Who is the next generation?

When I speak of the next generation of leaders, I am mostly referring to millennials, people who are ages twenty to thirty-six now in the second decade of the twenty-first century.[2] This generation roughly includes those born between 1980 and 2000. Soon these people will become America's largest living generation and hold the biggest share of the workforce. They'll be taking the reins in established leadership roles, but they are also creating new roles through online platforms and reimagined career possibilities.

Much has been written about millennials because they are so vastly different in life experience and perspective from previous generations. There's a lot of dialogue about millennials, but little conversation with and listening to millennials. Most millennials don't like the label *millennial* and distance themselves from that identity, believing that the name unfairly lumps them with a negative stereotype or perhaps creates a category that doesn't capture the variety and complexity of their experience. I get that. So for the next section, I'll simply use the term "the next generation" to delineate this subset of our society and then use the term *millennial* sparingly through the rest of the book. Here are a few characteristics that generally describe this upcoming generation of leaders.

1. The next generation is all about justice. This young generation has been unfairly characterized as self-absorbed and uncaring. I actually think that better describes my generation. Millennials have more truthfully been called *the justice generation* because of their tendency to act immediately when they see something wrong. They want to respond whether by doing an act of service, joining an online petition, or offering financial help. For some, the desire to help others comes from a religious motivation, but for many, it stems from a belief in the goodness of humans and the compassion to see that we're all hurting and needy. The justice generation is seeking to discover and save its own soul through acts of kindness without dealing with the attendant religious baggage. They embody the kind of faith that James, the brother of Jesus, taught: "Let us not love in word or talk but in deed and truth" (1 John 3:18, ESV).

2. The next generation is aware of the power and pervasiveness of terrorism. The most significant event for this generation is 9/11, when terrorists bombed the Twin Towers in New York. Security is a huge issue for millennials, not something to be taken for granted. They have never lived without a twenty-four-hour news cycle that constantly highlights the places in the world that are divided, desperate, and under siege. They don't just read about the schools where isolated teenagers and extremists walk in with an arsenal and commence random shootings. They have seen video of these events, watched interviews with those affected, and even attended those schools and experienced the fear personally.

3. *The next generation don't feel much economic security.* My daughter, who is fifteen, has some memory of the economic collapse of 2007 and 2008 and the anxiety that it caused families. We sold our home in 2010 after it was listed for more than two years on the market. She's attentive enough to know that there's no guarantee of a job after college and that perhaps the best route is to stay in school as long as possible to gain as much advantage as possible. Will there be jobs in the future, and do our current institutions prepare us for such jobs? Nothing is certain. No wonder there is so much focus on the immediate through social media. That's more tangible than what may happen five years from now. And why should millennials trust the generation of political leaders ahead of them when they've inherited a system with so many challenges?

4. *The next generation values multiracial perspectives.* My children have witnessed the first African-American president, who was elected on the hope that racism would finally be put to rest in America. There was great optimism that political divides could be overcome as racial tensions subsided. But after President Obama's eight years, the divide seems wider than ever, and communities are still segregated and suspicious of outsiders. Even so, millennials have never known a context that is not multiracial. They value the perspectives of different cultures and faiths. They are global in perspective, beyond national boundaries. They love their country, but they also see the good in other geographies, political systems, and customs.

5. *The next generation is connected 24/7.* Millennials know the power of technology, and the generation after them (Generation Y, those born after the year 2000) has always grown up with mobile technology. There is a world of knowledge at their fingertips. Got a question? Answers are available almost instantly. There are plenty of facts to sort through, and how those facts fit together in a consistent way of viewing the world can be challenging. The sharing of information is driving new possibilities of democratic reform in politically restrictive countries and helping nonprofits work together to create food security. Yet, oddly, the rise in mobile technology has also increased the amount of anxiety that people feel. People feel overwhelmed by the amount of information that comes into our field of vision each day. On the personal level, families can now know exactly where a child is, but we don't feel much safer. Instead, people feel more

fearful and even vulnerable if their cell phones aren't close by. With mobile technology, there is a constant stream of interactions and more anxiety about one's social standing, increasing our sense of disconnectedness. Even though people are sharing more personal information than ever before, there is a lurking sense that we can never know the true depth of another person—and that we will never fully be known either.

6. *The next generation values authenticity.* This may be the most defining quality of millennials. They value authentic exchanges. Inauthentic leaders repel them. They sense that there is more power in everyday, honest conversations than in a thousand political speeches. And they're right. Above all else, one must be true to oneself in the millennial generation.

7. *The next generation is spiritual but not religious.* There is a deep spiritual core in most millennials. They think deeply about the meaning of life and what it means to be human. I'm a big fan of the television show *The X-files.* Like Fox Mulder, the show's insistent searcher of the truth, *I want to believe.* I want to believe that we can do better. I want to believe that one day America will be a place that where racial differences aren't viewed as a problem to overcome but a diversity to be celebrated. I want to believe that every community can feel safe, where children are well fed and go to bed without the sound of gunshots. I want to believe that our senior adults can one day be cared for out of a deep sense of love and appreciation, living into old age surrounded by a community that values their lives. Most millennials, too, want to believe. But they want little to do with organized religion. They have been disappointed with the impotence of religion to bring about genuine change. Religion instead is viewed as the protector of the majority and as an arena that justifies racial separation and the poor treatment of gays, lesbians, and transgender people. If authenticity is the highest value of millennials, then religion has a real problem. Most congregations struggle to be places of authenticity and honest dialogue— and many fail—prompting most millennials to check out.

8. *The next generation is hopeful.* Amazingly, millennials describe themselves as hopeful and optimistic about the future. Even with the challenges ahead, they see a world of possibility. They just see it differently and have little expectation that the current structures can be reformed. They're imagining new ways of interacting, of doing business, of educating and cooperating. Many young people see a great future in giving their lives to businesses that make their communities better, working for nonprofits, or teaching in underserved areas to bring about a better future.

Martin Luther King Jr. said, "Everybody can be great . . . because anybody can serve. You don't have to have a college degree to serve. You don't have to make your subject and verb agree to serve. You only need a heart full of grace. A soul generated by love."[3]

The very qualities of authenticity, connectedness, and hopefulness give me great expectations for the kind of leaders that the next generation will be. Leaders who are justice minded and globally focused can transcend the boundaries and gridlock that currently define our politics. I'm hopeful that a better day is on the way. Just because the politics of the past have been defined by violence, divisiveness, and hatred doesn't mean our future has to be that way as well.

I was born in Birmingham, Alabama, just a few years before King delivered these words at Sixteenth Street Baptist Church in my hometown:

> The reason I can't follow the old eye-for-an-eye philosophy is that it ends up leaving everyone blind. Somebody must have sense and somebody must have religion. I remember some years ago, my brother and I were driving from Atlanta to Chattanooga, Tennessee. And for some reason the drivers that night were very discourteous or they were forgetting to dim their lights. . . . And finally A.D. looked over at me and he said, "I'm tired of this now, and the next car that comes by here and refuses to dim the lights, I'm going to refuse to dim mine." I said, "Wait a minute, don't do that. Somebody has to have some sense on this highway." And I'm saying the same thing for us here in Birmingham. We are moving up a mighty highway toward the city of Freedom. There will be meandering points. There will be curves and difficult moments, and we will be tempted to retaliate with the same kind of force that the opposition will use. But I'm going to say to you, "Wait a minute, Birmingham. Somebody's got to have some sense in Birmingham."[4]

How can we break the cycle of division and violence? How can we rise above the politics of anger and vitriol? I'm praying that the generation known as millennials will have more sense than my generation and that a wellspring of faith, hope, and love will rise up to help us become the community we know we can be.

This is a book for millennials, but it's also written to inspire and motivate anyone toward life-changing community engagement and toward reconsidering the politics we practice. In its three sections, "You," "Others," and "Politics," you'll read stories of faith, hope, and love, with each chapter dedicated to a truth we need to hear:

You

1. You'll need grit to have your voice heard (chutzpah).
2. You'll need humility to hear and value the voices of others (humility).
3. Your life is your message (authenticity).
4. You'll need an active inner life to balance an active outer life (introspection).
5. Vulnerability is strength, not weakness (vulnerability).

Others

6. No one story should dominate another (reverence).
7. We are more alike than we are different (mutuality).
8. People aren't meant to go it alone (togetherness).
9. We need to turn toward, not away from, those in need (compassion).
10. Small acts done in great love can change the world (blessing).

Politics

11. There is no magic bullet (tenacity).
12. Leaders must know what they believe in (faith).
13. Politics is sustained by hope (hope).
14. The end of politics is the beloved community (love).
15. We need people who will dream of a different world (imagination).

Notes

1. George Bernard Shaw, *Major Barbara* (1907), act 3.

2. Pew Research Center definition. See pewresearch.org/topics/millennials/.

3. Excerpted from "The Drum Major Instinct," a sermon by Rev. Martin Luther King, Jr., 1968, thekingcenter.org/get-involved#sthash.v9bW4rZL.dpuf.

4. Excerpted from "Love Your Enemies," a sermon preached by Rev. Martin Luther King, Jr., November 17, 1957, kingencyclopedia.stanford.edu/encyclopedia/documentsentry/doc_loving_your_enemies/.

Chapter 1

Chutzpah

There's no power in playing small, so get ready to rumble.

You're going to need some *chutzpah* in order to make a difference in the existing political, economic, and social practices of American life.

Chutzpah is true confidence and poise in the face of overwhelming challenges. It's shameless audacity, cheek, nerve, boldness, and temerity. Chutzpah is guts to push into hard situations and stay there long enough to see transformation happen. Experience is good. Practice, the 10,000-hours type, is necessary. But you'll also need some muscular, old-fashioned grit to make a difference.

The next generation of leaders will need to reckon with the powers that be if they're going to witness and participate in a more just and equitable America.

They'll need to stare down the elephant, remember the "why" of what's driving them into public life, and learn to summon the grit from a deep, personal reserve to make a real difference.

Staring Down the Elephant

After attending a peace conference in Zimbabwe that would jump-start my doctoral studies on the Rwandan genocide, I detoured to Kruger National Park in South Africa for a brief safari. Some of you may have seen the YouTube video called "The Battle at Kruger," an epic struggle between a herd of buffalo, a pride of lions, and two crocodiles. My experience at

Kruger proved just as intense and left me with a personal epic memory seared in my brain.

About thirty of us loaded into large, open vehicles for a night safari. Each of us had a spotlight that would catch the eyes of animals often hiding in dry riverbeds and savannas. For two hours we saw nothing except a glimpse of the uninspiring backside of a hippo. I had begun to think that we would not see anything as we started our journey back to the camp. But then we spotted two small elephants close to the road on the right and quickly came to a stop. Baby elephants are remarkably cute, and every face was turned as we snapped pictures and felt fortunate to be that close to the animals.

All of a sudden we heard a blood-curdling screech from the other side. Every head turned to see a massive mother elephant emerging from the brush and rushing our vehicle. We had split the herd as they were crossing the road. Other elephants could be seen close behind the mother. Everyone in the vehicle screamed as the car lurched forward and the elephant rolled left to pursue us. I was in the backseat of the vehicle, totally powerless to do anything about our situation. I felt helpless and terrified.

And this is the memory now seared in my brain: a huge head slightly turned down, barreling toward us like a bull, ears flapping out and trunk swinging wildly. It was less than ten feet from the car and approaching fast.

The guide gunned the engine with the elephant in pursuit. Thankfully, as we pulled farther ahead, the animal began to slow and eventually turned back to her babies. Then the guide did something strange: he pulled just a little farther ahead and stopped the car. We watched as the elephant comforted her babies with one eye on us, occasionally pawing at the ground in our direction and waving her ears. We had narrowly escaped, and now the driver was inviting a second brush with danger. Those in the car were still frightened and urged the driver to move on. He calmly told us that only once in his twenty-five years of guiding safaris had an elephant struck one of his vehicles, and that was just a glancing brush.

We waited a while longer and then drove back to the camp. There was no more spotlighting, no more searching. We had witnessed something that would never be forgotten. No one said a word as we drove back to camp, as lingering terror and relief and thrill compressed into a strange silence.

That story represents what many of us in America feel: caught in the middle. We feel powerless, stuck in the backseat with someone else driving, moving in a direction we don't want to go. If anything unites us today, it is the feeling of powerlessness. It often feels like power is somewhere else than where we are.

Donald Trump tapped into this feeling of powerlessness in the 2016 United States presidential campaign. In the essay, "Is There Too Much or Too Little Democracy in America?" Michael Lind cites a 2016 survey by the RAND Corporation that reported the single factor that best predicted voter support for Donald Trump among likely Republican voters. It wasn't income, education, race, gender, or attitudes toward Muslims or immigrants. The single greatest predictor was agreement with the statement, "People like me don't have any say."[1]

Those who feel like their power is threatened or has already been taken choose a range of responses. Some retreat. Some become cynical and bitter. And some fight back, even though they're not even sure where to place their anger. They give in to the politics of polarization, where there are only winners and losers, enemies and friends.

But perhaps there is a better posture. Like our guide with the elephant, perhaps there's room to face the climate of hopelessness and powerlessness with chutzpah, without giving in or giving up.

How are we to respond to the politics of division and polarization?

First, we can seize this moment to embrace a more egalitarian approach to politics. The fissure in American politics is real and wide, but it is not impassable. We need to take seriously those who feel like they have no power as well as those who have historically been kept from the table of decision-making. Who feels disenfranchised? Why do they feel neglected or unheard? If our community organizations, neighborhoods, and churches can't honor those who feel marginalized and pushed aside, we have little hope to dissuade them from angry and divisive attitudes and responses.

At the height of the Civil Rights struggle in 1968, Martin Luther King, Jr., said,

> It is not enough for me to stand before you tonight and condemn riots. It would be morally irresponsible for me to do that without, at the same time, condemning the contingent, intolerable conditions that exist in our society. These conditions are the things that cause individuals to feel that they have no other alternative than to engage in violent rebellions to get attention. And I must say tonight that a riot is the language of the unheard.[2]

Are you tired of divisive politics? Now is the time to gather people together across racial and ideological lines and hear one another. Dialogue is good, but a specific kind of talk is necessary. We need to talk about the past. How do others perceive history? Where do others perceive injustice, then and now?

Second, we can become more contemplative. Rather than joining the chorus of criticism and division, we can take time to still our voices and meditate on how things have become this caustic. For religious people, this may mean prayer. Prayer has always been a source of power for those who believe in God. For those who are not religious, this may mean meditation on great writings, poetry, or principles and values. If we feel powerless, then, rather than ranting and pointing fingers, we can pause.

The courage to speak up is critical. But it also takes courage to be silent and listen.

Not long ago, our church organized a conversation between Christians and Muslims. Fifty Christians and fifty Muslims sat down for a meal together with a set of questions and possible conversation directions. We talked about things like faith traditions and practices but also about family, media perceptions, and community concerns like the safety of our children. At the end, we opened the floor for comments on what people had learned. While many talked about how they learned things about religious beliefs, one elderly gentleman offered this: "The more I talked to my new friend, the more I liked him." That kind of perspective only comes through listening.

All types of dialogue groups are springing up within communities that have two things in common: a shared meal and a guided conversation. These conversations have real power. They level the playing field and invite people to suspend judgment for a while, opting simply to listen to points of view that may be different from theirs. Our state and national politics could learn a lot from those who are engaging in intentional table fellowship.

Finally, we can become more active. We can engage in tangible and symbolic acts of service together. The antidote to powerlessness is to get moving and create some powerful inertia in a positive direction that will last long after the screams of a political rally die down.

We can't stay stuck in the backseat, powerless and terrified. We have to get active. Our democracy demands a constant, active, and thoughtful engagement with our most cherished principles that leads to real action. And we can't wait to get active until the day when politics are different.

Our tendency may be to want to shrink from these challenges, but I believe that we need more chutzpah as demonstrated by my safari guide that night. We need young people who will stare down these challenges and redefine what civic engagement looks like—that is, not driven by money and power interests but instead by love for one's neighbor and a desire to see all boats lifted, for, as the aphorism says, "A rising tide lifts all boats."

Remembering the "Why"

When the going gets tough, remembering the "why" behind what you're doing makes all the difference.

I've always been interested in political races, but in 2007, I was able to hear and meet presidential or vice presidential candidates or office holders up close and personal. During that election cycle, I was either invited to attend or took my own initiative to see Dick Cheney, Hillary Clinton, Mike Huckabee, and Barack Obama. It was fascinating to hear their different political perspectives and witness the energy surrounding these personalities.

I had also just taken a job as a religious denominational leader that gave me a quasi-public role. I represented and served churches with members across the political spectrum.

For the most part, I was able to fly under the radar for these events. But when I met Barack Obama, afterwards I was asked unexpectedly by a television crew to offer a few thoughts on his rally. So I gave my impressions and thought it unlikely that anyone would notice.

That was a foolish assumption.

Even though I had attended several other rallies for Republicans and Democrats, just being present at the Obama rally and giving a positive word about the enthusiasm of the crowd invoked an incredible backlash. I received emails and phone calls from friends who saw the news and couldn't believe that I would be present at such an event. People questioned whether I could effectively lead a state religious organization if I was so passionate about one party and especially about one candidate. It made little difference when I explained how I voted for the person, not the party, and that I was just exploring each candidate's position on the issues.

I learned a lot from that experience. It was instructive how quickly misunderstanding can arise and how social dynamics can keep individuals and leaders from speaking out. I was awakened to how passionate people can be about their own political positions.

But it also exposed two fundamental questions that I still wrestle with: First, what does it really mean to be politically active as a person of faith? And second, what am I truly passionate about in politics that would lead me beyond a spectator position and into real action?

Rallies are all about a candidate sharing views and trying to whip up enthusiasm. They're fun (some would say), but little of practical value is accomplished. The speeches stay the same from state to state, and candidates rarely remain in one place for more than a few hours and a few fund-raisers.

For citizens, what matters more than showing up for a rally, getting on television in support of a candidate, or even putting up a sign in your yard is the way you display an active pursuit of the political issues that matter most to you.

Fortunately, I had quite a bit of latitude in the way I could organize events for our congregations that weren't overtly political. We tried to speak to issues of significance, such as the UN Millennium Development Goals: the environment, safety for children who had been abused, justice in the prison system, racial reconciliation, and alleviation of poverty. We invited political leaders, state and local law enforcement, and other civic and religious leaders to speak on community issues.

Through all of these efforts, I was expressing something about what I believed. I was discovering that I was passionate about helping those who feel excluded to connect to real relationships. I've also got passion for racial reconciliation and especially for helping vulnerable women and children. Lots of important causes deserve attention—the environment, human trafficking, poverty, homelessness, the mentally ill—but the plight of the lonely, racially divided, and vulnerable really makes my heart beat faster.

What gives you passion? What makes your heart beat faster?

It's a good practice to write down what you believe, why you believe it, and what you want to see accomplished because of that belief.

Most people don't know the "why" underneath what they believe and what they do.

This past year, I began to get more intentional about setting goals and sticking to them. I set these goals based on what I believed and what I felt like I could accomplish in one year to further my impact in these areas. I took a few days and worked through the crafting of a vision, attainable goals, and action steps for the upcoming year. It felt great to commit these goals to paper.

But then the inevitable happened. The initial excitement died down, and the hard work began of actually accomplishing the goals, piece by piece. Fortunately, someone suggested to me at the beginning of the process that I not only write down each goal but also write down *why* I want to accomplish each goal. What will be the benefits of achieving each goal? What will happen if I *don't* reach each goal? How will I feel if I succeed? How will I feel if I fail? When I feel discouraged now, I read what drove me to set the goal in the first place.

Writing out the "why" for what you believe and the goals you want to accomplish will help you to persevere when you want to quit. It can serve to remind you of what you believe and why you do what you do. It's an important part of grit.

Summoning the Grit

But where does grit come from? And can a person develop grit if they think they are lacking?

The greatest thrill and glory of a football player is to play in the Super Bowl. And the greatest accomplishment for NFL players is to be able to wear the Super Bowl championship ring and stand with their team on the victory podium. Players are willing to give their all to achieve that moment of victory.

Not long ago I watched the movie *Concussion*, which is about the brain damage caused by repeatedly being hit in the head in football. Some players have said that it's like running into a brick wall again and again. And in spite of their incredible conditioning, just about every NFL player is suffering with or recovering from some kind of injury.

You have to ask, *why do these players do this?* Why would they subject their bodies again and again to this punishment? Where do they summon the grit to keep going? Some play for money, but most would say that they play for the love of the game and the drive toward victory. Even though they have to suffer, they keep going because they believe it's absolutely worth it.

Grit is defined as "perseverance and passion for long-term goals."[3] Grit begins with passion—the love of the game or politics or relationships or business—and is sustained by a deeply personal motivation.

Angela Duckworth has pioneered research in the area of personal motivation and perseverance. Her studies have focused on the question, why do some people accomplish more than others? What leads to exceptional achievement? She has identified five qualities that mark those with grit.[4]

1. Courage

This is the capacity that someone has to manage fear, especially the fear of failure. Courage may be hard to measure, but it's definitely a quality to develop, and it's directly proportional to how much grit you have. Courage means that as you do all you can to succeed, you don't let your fear of crashing and burning stop you. Stumbling, failing, making mistakes, looking and feeling stupid are all part of the process, not enemies of your success. We learn valuable lessons when we suffer defeat, perhaps more valuable than what we learn when we succeed.

Teddy Roosevelt addressed the necessity of overcoming fear and managing vulnerability in an speech he made at the Sorbonne in 1907. My dad used to have this quote from Roosevelt's speech on his office wall, and now it's on my wall:

> It is not the critic who counts; not the man who points out how the strong man stumbles, or where the doer of deeds could have done better. The credit belongs to the man who is actually in the arena, whose face is marred by dust and sweat and blood; who strived valiantly; who errs, who comes again and again, because there is no effort without error and shortcoming; but who does actually strive to do the deeds; who knows great enthusiasms, the great devotions; who spends himself in a worthy cause; who at the best knows in the end the triumph of high achievement, and who at the worst, if he fails, at least fails while daring greatly.

Fear of failure can paralyze us. But when we have a mindset that failure is just part of the process that leads to success, our courage begins to build.

2. Conscientiousness

To be conscientious is to seek to do your job well. It's a steady job accomplished with attention and hard work. No matter what he or she feels on any given day (and we all have good days and bad days), the conscientious person keeps showing up, demonstrating a dependable demeanor and a willingness to work hard.

One can't just be dependable, however, if one wants to achieve great change. There still must be passion and a willingness to do things out of the box, in a new and unexpected way. Being self-controlled is essential, but sometimes self-control and conventionality go against the essence of grit.

3. Endurance

I often have shared with my son and daughter that 90 percent of success is just showing up. To transform American politics to a more egalitarian, just, and participative process, we need young people who will serve for the long haul. Writer Eugene Peterson calls the idea of perseverance, or endurance, "a long obedience in the same direction."[5]

4. Resilience

Resilience involves optimism, creativity, and confidence no matter how bad things get. It's the ability to get back on your feet, and it's not just for individuals. Teams can show resilience. Communities and even nations can demonstrate the capacity to pick themselves up and keep moving forward, remaining true to their core beliefs and integrity.

Resilience could be defined as the capacity of people, communities, and societal systems to sustain their central purpose and integrity in the midst of change and crisis. Those who consistently model resilience see their lives as having purpose, believe that they can make a difference and effect change, and use positive and negative experiences to grow and learn.

5. Excellence

Striving for excellence is different from working for perfection. With perfection, there is no middle ground. Stumbling or failing is not an option. What matters the most is reaching some standard of accomplishment, which is often subjective. On the other hand, excellence is a state of mind. The word *excellence* is derived from the Greek word *arête*, which suggests the fulfillment of purpose or function and is closely associated with virtue. It's about progress and moving toward the goal of being the best one can be. Striving for excellence means embracing failure, vulnerability, and disappointment in the quest for improvement.

While some people seem more naturally courageous, resilient, and so on, it's important to remember that what these qualities look like in one person may be different for another. It may be an act of courage for you to stand and make a speech, while for another person doing so would be no big deal. For that person, having the courage to identify with and volunteer for a community organization may be a huge growth step.

We'll become defeated if we're always measuring ourselves against others. All we can do is seek to become the best selves we can be and to make strides in the direction of courage, conscientiousness, endurance, resilience, and excellence.

It can also be defeating if one looks at these qualities and immediately makes an assessment of how little or how much one has. But when you believe that you can grow, and that over time you can become the leader you know you can be, then you'll see that you really can develop grit.

Terry Tempest Williams said,

> The human heart is the first home of democracy. It is where we embrace our questions. Can we be equitable? Can we be generous? Can we listen with our whole beings, not just our minds, and offer our attention rather than our opinions? And do we have enough resolve in our hearts to act courageously, relentlessly, without giving up—ever—trusting our fellow citizens to join with us in our determined pursuit of a living democracy?[6]

If you want to pursue a living democracy, you're going to need resolve, courage, chutzpah. Our communities and our nation need you to have it.

Notes

1. Michael Lind, "Is There Too Much or Too Little Democracy in America?" *The New York Times*, May 14, 2016.

2. Dr. Martin Luther King, Jr., "The Other America," speech delivered at Grosse Pointe High School, March 14, 1968, gphistorical.org/mlk/mlkspeech/index.htm.

3. A. L. Duckworth, C. Peterson, M. D. Matthews, and D. R. Kelly, "Grit: Perseverance and Passion for Long-term Goals," *Journal of Personality and Social Psychology* 92/6 (2007): 1087.

4. Cited in Margaret M. Perlis, "5 Characteristics of Grit—How Many Do You Have?" *Forbes*, October 29, 2013, forbes.com/sites/margaretperlis/2013/10/29/5-characteristics-of-grit-what-it-is-why-you-need-it-and-do-you-have-it/#2c2929ce4f7b.

5. See his book, *Perseverance: A Long Obedience in the Same Direction*, published in 1996.

6. Terry Tempest Williams, "Engagement," *Orion Magazine*, orionmagazine.org/article/engagement/.

Chapter 2

Humility

Achievement and ambition need the tempering of the inner life of humility.

After chutzpah comes humility. Or maybe it's the other way around.

On the road to becoming one of the most celebrated Americans of all time, Benjamin Franklin believed that he was falling short as a human being. His external scorecard was already impressive as a young man—he was an inventor, writer, and publisher before the age of twenty—but his internal scorecard revealed a person who was disordered, undisciplined, and failing in many ways.

Franklin concocted a project he called "moral perfection." He listed twelve areas of attitude and conduct that needed improvement and decided to read the list each day and focus on a different virtue each week, repeating the process until he had achieved his measure of the virtue. He then asked a friend to look over his list.

Franklin said that his friend "kindly informed me that I was generally thought proud; that my pride showed itself frequently in conversation." He was told that he was lacking an essential, thirteenth virtue: humility.[1]

Of course, it's hard to work on being humble; the very act makes you suspect. Anyone who says, "I'm becoming more humble," well, isn't.

But Franklin's effort paid off. He rightly identified his quest for "moral perfection" as a future effort. Instead, he began to focus more on kindness, forbearance, and a willingness to listen. Later in his life he would write, "Be at war with your vices, at peace with your neighbors, and let every new year find you a better man."

By the time the 1787 Constitutional Convention met in Philadelphia, Franklin was the most respected and elderly delegate (at eighty-one years old). He had been critical of some of the writing of the Constitution, knowing that it would need amendments and would ultimately be hard to sustain as a governing document. Even so, on the last day of the Convention, he stated, "The older I grow, the more apt I am to doubt my own judgment, and to pay more respect to the judgment of others." Franklin asked each person "to doubt a little of his own infallibility" and recommended that the Convention vote unanimously in favor of the document.[2]

It seems like he found success in that thirteenth virtue after all. Franklin's inner scorecard (the measure of his character, moderation, sincerity, sense of justice, and so on) is as much remembered as his external scorecard (his successes as an inventor, writer, publisher, politician, and writer).

In *Good to Great*, Jim Collins makes the case that the top leaders, the ones he calls "level 5 leaders," practice a balance of professional drive with deep humility. These leaders embody an incredible force of ambition and achievement, but they temper their inner fire with humility such that the larger goals of their fellow workers and the overall organization can be accomplished. They keep their egos and potential arrogance in check for the greater good.

But what does humility look like?

Humility means listening to others and seeking to understand. Arrogance demands to be heard and understood.

Humility means that you can say, "I was wrong" and "I'm sorry." Arrogance views such statements as weakness or an unnecessary activity.

Humility means that you stay open to fresh ideas, including those from others, and have a willingness to learn something new. Arrogance demonstrates a posture that says, "I know best."

Humility means that you celebrate when others find success. Arrogance leaves one feeling diminished when others do something good, as if there's only so much achievement to be had in the world.

Humility means that you find ways to put others in the spotlight. Arrogance wants all the light for oneself.

Humility means that you seek the happiness and comfort of others. Arrogance demands that you always get your way, becoming irritable and abrasive when you don't.

Humility means knowing when you need help and asking for it, with a true perception of your strengths and weaknesses. Arrogance prefers to go it alone, refusing to admit one's inadequacy and dependence on others.

Humility means resisting the opportunity to humiliate and punish your enemy when they find themselves in a powerless position. Arrogance strikes at that moment for personal gain.

Humility means giving power away when there's plenty to share. Arrogance grasps for power in a zero-sum game.

Humility means practicing quiet strength when circumstances are difficult. Arrogance seeks to control, manipulate, and dominate when times get tough.

Quiet Strength

Quiet, selfless strength holds more power than blustering brashness.

Just a few miles from my childhood home in Montgomery, Alabama, one of the greatest acts of political courage in America's history took place. An unlikely, weary, solitary woman would shake the soul of a nation and inspire a community.

On June 15, 1999, the Congressional Medal of Honor was given to Mrs. Rosa Parks. But she wasn't thinking about awards or starting a revolution when, on December 1, 1955, she refused to move to the back of a city bus.

A longtime activist and secretary of the local NAACP chapter, Parks was traveling home on the bus when, as more whites boarded, she was ordered to give up her seat so a white man could sit down. She refused and was arrested.

There are mixed accounts about her motives. Was she just tired from a long day? Parks herself said that particular day was no different from other days when she was weary from work. Instead, Parks said that the only thing she was tired of was "taking it." She had always nurtured a rebellious streak because she was a black woman living in a white man's society. On that day, she was soul-weary, angry at the injustice of having to relinquish her seat so that another person could sit down.

50,000 other African-Americans would join her in boycotting city buses. The nation witnessed their quiet courage and willingness to sacrifice—often losing sleep and walking many miles to continue their work.

And it all started with an introverted, steady servant.

Rosa Parks was frequently perceived as a forceful, prophetic woman with a bold personality, someone who could take a stand even in the face of a dangerous, crowded busload of opponents. But when she passed away in 2005 at the age of ninety-two, she was described again and again as soft-spoken, even-tempered, and reticent. Parks was timid and shy but also courageous. Her obituaries and letters of appreciation upon her death were full of phrases like "radical humility" and "quiet fortitude." She didn't raise her voice often, but when she spoke, people listened.

Amy Black said in her blog post "Radical Humility in Everyday Politics," "In our bombastic and high-volume media age, it is tempting to think that the intensity of our tone is the best way to demonstrate the sincerity of our beliefs and values."[3]

Rosa Parks demonstrated that there was a different way. Isn't that what people are yearning for—not more of the same, but a different way of interacting with one another? Humility requires more courage than free-wielding power, because it involves giving power away. Humility is chutzpah combined with compassion and service.

Humility in American Political Life

I wouldn't be writing this chapter if I didn't believe humility is absolutely essential in American political life. But many people have come to question how much we can really expect from leaders. Is humility a bygone mark of civility from a different era? I want to suggest that, in order to see a more robust culture of humility in public life, we need to recognize that (1) there is already of wealth of humility among our leaders that needs to be celebrated, and (2) we need to start with ourselves if we want to see more humility infused into our political process.

Whereas chutzpah is highly valued in public leaders, humility is grossly undervalued.

Humility can help you relate to people better, become a more effective public servant, and allow you to sleep better at night, but it won't get you much attention in the media. Media-grabbing and stinger tweets on Twitter get attention. But that's not the whole story.

While quiet, humble acts don't get much media attention, each day there are thousands of quiet public servants, county commissioners, tax assessors, probate court and family court officials, administrative government workers, Congressmen and Congresswomen, and many other leaders who know that it is better to serve than to be served, better to give than to receive.

I know dozens of leaders in the city where I live (Dallas) and hundreds of others from my experiences growing up that lead me to believe humility is more common than we think.

One of my mentors from is a great man named John Baker. He was elected to the Alabama Legislature at a young age and served with integrity, recognized as the Outstanding Young Legislator one year and eventually becoming the chairman of the Alabama Democratic Party from 1984–1991. He went on to be a lobbyist for Norfolk Railroad and continued to be politically connected in many ways. He showed persistence, optimism, and grit in the time that he worked to make the state of Alabama a better place. But what I value most in him is the humility I saw firsthand, especially in his willingness to spend time with me. It was his influence that cultivated my love for politics and for people of all kinds.

I think too of my friend Harold Phillips who has served in the Liberty, Missouri City Council for many years in addition to his day job as a religious leader. He has a quick wit, an easy style, and a heart to help others. He's making Liberty a good place to live through his natural talents and heart for service.

I think of my friend David Greene, the mayor of Duncanville, Texas. His position is not salaried, but the difference he makes for the city of Duncanville is huge. He loves people, knows how to get things done, and works hard for Duncanville.

The common thread that runs through each of these examples is humility, although each person would be quick to deny that quality.

We need to celebrate examples like these more. I could point you to many other people in the city of Dallas who serve not from a place of pride and expectation of appreciation and reward but out of a love for people and a sincere desire to make our city a better place. We need to recognize that humility has been a significant mark of our political leaders from the early days with leaders like Benjamin Franklin and persisting until today. When we have this mindset of expecting our leaders to be humble and service oriented in their actions, we'll get more leaders who mirror those qualities.

But we can't expect of our leaders what we do not practice ourselves.

I believe that our politics are no better than our populace. There have always been cases where a few people sour the whole political experience for others, but by and large we get the politics we deserve. If someone becomes popular through divisive, bigotry-fueled language, that person stands before an army of like-minded people making him or her popular. If someone becomes embroiled in corruption and scandal, it's likely that the populace wasn't watching or engaged enough before it was too late, or perhaps we liked the successes the person was achieving too much to care.

Mahatma Gandhi said,

> We but mirror the world. All the tendencies present in the outer world are to be found in the world of our body. If we could change ourselves, the tendencies in the world would also change. As a man changes his own nature, so does the attitude of the world change towards him. This is the divine mystery supreme. A wonderful thing it is and the source of our happiness. We need not wait to see what others do.[4]

To transform a culture, first seek to be transformed yourself. To see more profound, humble service in political life, then "be the change you want to see," as Gandhi's words are often paraphrased.

Cultivating Humility

As Benjamin Franklin's life revealed, humility is developed over a lifetime. Like a well-cultivated garden, years of digging in the dirt of your own failures, planting simple acts of serving others, weeding out bad habits, and watering through the study of humble examples such as Rosa Parks can lead to a life of beauty.

Here are three ideas for cultivating humility.

Be ready to admit your mistakes. When you win, win quietly and point to the efforts of others. Don't call attention to yourself all the time. Instead, affirm the ways in which you have failed, and learn to laugh and gain perspective from those mistakes. It takes courage to be vulnerable about your failures. Be quick to share how you may have let yourself down, and let that serve as a lesson to others. This isn't self-hatred but a healthy, honest view of yourself, including your faults as well as your strengths.

Learn to appreciate the efforts of others. Others don't exist to be manipulated for your particular needs and ends. It's a great gift to share our lives with others, and a great leader knows how to appreciate the gifts that others bring into the world. Say thanks regularly, with a sincere heart.

Practice a different posture toward your enemies when they experience failure. Matthew Dowd said, "The greatest power of humility in bringing positive change to our world exists when a leader brings opponents in when he is strong, gives power away when he has plenty, and lifts up the enemy with a strong and compassionate hand. The true measure of humility is the exercise of it when a leader has won, is strong and on top, not when they have lost and are weak and down."[5]

When you learn to live with confidence and humility, with a mature sense of your own strengths and weaknesses and an appreciation for the gifts and struggles of others, you'll become an uncommon leader.

Mother Teresa demonstrated that kind of uncommon life. In humility, she served the poor in Calcutta, India, for many decades, but she also gained international attention as a voice for the poor and oppressed. Tony Campolo tells about a time when Mother Teresa was visiting the United States and heard about a crisis in a small Pennsylvanian town.[6]

A local state hospital that took care of those suffering from psychiatric illnesses wanted to establish a safe house in which people could live for a time to be restored back into the community after a mental health crisis. The plan was to create a residence with continued treatment and services in order to help people return from isolation into the mainstream.

When some people living in the town heard about this plan, they began to actively advocate against those "crazy" folks coming to live in their neighborhood. They appealed to the city council. On the night of the vote, the place was packed. Five hundred people squeezed into the hall, yelling and screaming their opposition to the halfway houses, while television cameras reported the event. Without much discussion, the council voted unanimously not to allow the residence to be established.

Not long after the vote, the back doors of the auditorium burst open, and in walked Mother Teresa. She happened to be in town for a benefit for the Sisters of Charity program and had heard about the vote. She strode down the center aisle and the crowd hushed and gasped as they realized who she was. Before the city council, Mother Teresa fell to her knees and begged the city council to provide a space for the mentally ill in their community. She lifted her arms and said, "In the name of Jesus, make room for these children of God! When you reject them, you reject Jesus. When you affirm them, you embrace Jesus." And then, with her arms upraised, five times in a row she said, "Please, please, please, please, please, in the name of God, make room for these people! Make room for them in your neighborhoods."

The cameras kept rolling, and Mother Teresa stayed on her knees, awaiting a response. Finally one of the city council members said, "I move we change the decision." Another council member seconded the motion, and they voted unanimously to reverse the decision they had just made. It was reported that among the 500 in attendance, not one spoke a word of opposition to the motion.

What had happened? It's simple, really. Mother Teresa, who held such credibility through acts of love and humility, had spoken up on behalf of others and appealed to the townspeople's better selves. On the streets of Calcutta, she sacrificed herself each day on behalf of the poor, and through her humility she had gained a power that was greater than any military, political, social, or economic might.

That's how you can cultivate humility: by caring for others, by being your genuine self with all your flaws and beauty, by advocating for others and not for yourself.

On the day of his resignation as the Speaker of the House of the United States House of Representatives, John Boehner read this prayer attributed to St. Francis of Assisi:

Lord, make me an instrument of thy peace.
Where there is hatred, let me sow love;
Where there is injury, pardon;
Where there is doubt, faith;
Where there is despair, hope;
Where there is darkness, light;
Where there is sadness, joy.
O divine Master, grant that I may not so much seek
To be consoled as to console,
To be understood as to understand,
To be loved as to love;
For it is in giving that we receive;
It is in pardoning that we are pardoned;
It is in dying to self that we are born to eternal life.[7]

Notes

1. Check out Franklin's thirteen virtues at thirteenvirtues.com.

2. Derek A. Webb, "Doubting a Little of One's Infallibility: The Real Miracle at Philadelphia," *Constitution Daily* (Blog), January 18, 2013, constitutioncenter.org/blog/doubting-a-little-of-ones-infallibility-the-real-miracle-at-philadelphia.

3. Amy Black, "Radical Humility in Everyday Politics: Christian Humility in the American Political Circus," *The Table* (Blog), July 1, 2016, cct.biola.edu/adding-much-needed-dose-humility-politics/.

4. Originally printed in *Indian Opinion*, 1913, reprinted in M. Gandhi, *The Collected Works of M.K. Gandhi*, vol. 13, ch. 153 (New Delhi, India: The Publications Division, 1960) 241.

5. Matthew Dowd, "A Leadership and Life Model Based on Humility," last modified November 18, 2013, abcnews.go.com/Politics/leadership-life-model-based-humility/story?id=20926911.

6. Tony Campolo, "Earning the Right to Be Heard," Program 5218, February 8, 2009.

7. For the origin of this prayer, see franciscan-archive.org/franciscana/peace.html.

Chapter 3

Authenticity

You're always telling your story.

I heard about a young man named Justin who quit his job. It was a flexible, well-paying job, but Justin said he just couldn't take it anymore. He had moved to Hollywood as an aspiring actor in search of his dream. While working for his big break, he waited tables at a high-end restaurant that attracted lots of celebrities. Huge checks led to huge tips. Also, the managers at the restaurant showed flexibility when someone had an audition and needed to leave quickly or show up late. Studio executives, casting directors, and agents flocked to the restaurant, increasing an aspiring actor's chance of being discovered.

Justin's friend who often went to the restaurant asked why he would quit such a great job. Was it a long drive or a bad supervisor?

"I just couldn't do the water," Justin said. His friend looked at him, confused.

"We charge for water," he continued. "If you ask for water, I am supposed to ask if you want bottled or sparkling. If they choose bottled, I bring out a big bottle and explain it is sourced from an aquifer in Sweden with a depth of 1,500 feet. So fresh and clean, it is untouched even by air until it gets harvested and bottled. It is $25 a bottle."

"OK," the friend wondered. "What's the big deal, if they're rich people on corporate work accounts? So what?"

"It's not true," Justin said.

"Well, I'm sure it's not 1,500 feet or whatever in Sweden, but—"

"No, none of it is true."

Justin explained that the restaurant bought around thirty bottles of the high-end bottled water brand. When someone ordered the bottled water, the job of the waiter was to take one of the empty bottles, fill it with tap water, and then serve it.

"Haven't you ever noticed the cap is always off when we set the bottle down?" Justin inquired. The friend thought about it and remembered that yes, the bottle was always presented with the cap off.

"I just couldn't do it anymore. I felt so scummy lying to people," Justin said. "There were lots of other things like that about the restaurant, but the water was the final straw. Charging $25 for tap water and passing it off as imported bottled water was the last straw. I couldn't do it anymore, so I quit."

"And no one ever caught on?" the friend asked.

"Nope. It's Hollywood, man. People look at the label; they don't care about what's inside."

Justin's observation could well characterize much of American culture. Obsessed with brands and image, the millennial generation is especially marketed to with a deft, subtle message that genuineness matters above all ("be true to yourself") but that identification with certain products and services is the only way to truly be you. Our Facebook pages offer the self we want to be, not necessarily the self we truly are. As long as the bottle looks fine, what difference does the nature of the water make?

What would have happened if Justin had continued to sell the "bottled" water, knowing it was a sham? What would that have done to his soul over time? In many ways, his life would have become like what he was asked to do at work: a presentation of an outer shell that didn't represent his inner life.

Often people try to live life in reverse. They believe that if they have more external resources, more things, an abundance of everything to make them happy, then their inner lives will be fulfilled. The opposite is true. We must first be who we truly are on the inside, and then we can discover what we need to do out of that sacred center in order to gather what we may want.

Who we are on the inside and who we are on the outside must be consistent. That is the nature of genuineness. Another name for genuineness is authenticity. To be truly what one claims to be doesn't come naturally in a culture obsessed with the exterior more than the interior, but the good news is that it can be intentionally cultivated. Authenticity is a choice, and it's a hard one.

e. e. cummings wrote, "To be nobody but yourself in a world which is doing its best, night and day, to make you everybody but yourself—means to fight the hardest battle which any human being can fight—and never stop fighting."[1]

Brené Brown says this about authenticity:

Authenticity is the daily practice of letting go of who we think we're supposed to be and embracing who we are. Choosing authenticity means: cultivating the courage to be imperfect, to set boundaries, and to allow ourselves to be vulnerable; exercising the compassion that comes from knowing that we are all made of strength and struggle; and nurturing the connection and sense of belonging that can only happen when we believe that we are enough. Authenticity demands wholehearted living and loving—even when it's hard, even when we're wrestling with the shame and fear of not being good enough, and especially when the joy is so intense that we're afraid to let ourselves feel it. Mindfully practicing authenticity during our most soul-searching struggles is how we invite grace, joy, and gratitude into our lives.[2]

While authenticity involves wrestling with oneself about fears and shame, the payoff for such soul-work is priceless. It leads to true connection. When you encounter someone who is really authentic, it's often the most memorable quality you remember about them.

Authenticity, Actually

I often encounter people who have misconceptions about what it means to be authentic. Does it mean always speaking what you are thinking, in every moment, regardless of how it might hurt someone? Does it mean continuing to be a jerk to others, excusing yourself with the mantra, "This is who I am"?

"Be true to yourself" may be the closest creedal statement that millennials can make. There's no greater sin, some claim, than to hide who you really are. But what does an authentic life look like?

Psychotherapist Amy Morin has identified three myths about authenticity that actually hinder us from living a truly genuine life.[3] Those who cling to these beliefs will likely never truly live with authenticity.

The first myth is that being comfortable in one's skin equates to always acting the same in every circumstance. For instance, if you're thinking something in the privacy of your head, then it's appropriate to share publicly (such as on Facebook) everything you think. It may be something you could or should share, but that doesn't mean you ought to share it on social media outlets in the name of authenticity. I can be who I am without sharing every thought for my mom to see, and it's not necessary for her to know my every thought in order to know who I am.

Similarly, when interviewing for a job, you may selectively convey parts of yourself to benefit your chances of being hired. We all have areas of shame due to mistakes and failures that aren't necessary to convey in every moment. We should not portray ourselves to be what we are not, but authenticity doesn't demand always speaking our minds or acting the same way no matter the situation.

The second myth is that one's values are static, never changing. The truth is that who I am at this stage of life is different than who I was fifteen years ago, and that's how it should be. We should always be learning, growing, adapting, and adjusting as life brings us highs and lows. Being authentic doesn't mean we won't contradict ourselves from time to time or that we will never change our minds.

The third myth is that being authentic means that one should be brutally honest all the time. This requires the sacrifice of kindness and wisdom for the sake of genuineness. Demonstrating kindness, however, is just as important as speaking authentically.

So what does authenticity look like? It is a life that holds in tension the genuineness and truth of oneself with forbearance and love toward others. Only when we walk with a posture of goodness and thoughtfulness toward others can we expect for them to be truly authentic around us.

The truth is that our lives speak volumes. The words we use and the way we treat others reveals what is within our souls. Genuineness, ideally, is a quality that leads us to become more and more gracious and kind. Some people are authentic but not kind; others may be kind within but fake toward anyone else. An exterior, genuine life that reveals an interior goodness is remarkable and compelling.

Your Life Is Your Message

Which matters more, the inside or the outside? A genuine life suggests the cultivation of a both/and dynamic.

Let's flip the water analogy. Imagine that you're thirsty. *Really thirsty.* And someone comes along and offers you a bottle of crystal-clear, cold water.

Before they put it in your hands, though, they dip the water bottle in a toilet. Now it's disgusting. It doesn't look as appealing as it did earlier.

The person offering it to you pleads, "But the water is good. It's clean and safe to drink. The outside may be awful, but don't think about the container. Just think about the purity of the water and how good it's going to taste."

Would you take the bottle of water? You would likely say, "No thanks."

You may know in your mind that the water is clear and safe and refreshing, but because the container is dirty, you perceive that the water inside may be contaminated, too. If you reject the water, you're affirming that the bottle that delivers the water matters as much as the water.

In the same way, your life affects your message. As a container, your life needs to reflect the purity and integrity of the thing you are offering. Your exterior life can either undermine the message or enhance—in a sense, "sell"—the message.

You likely have big dreams. You may want to make a difference in the lives of children, teaching content, skills, and character that will last a lifetime. You may want to own a business that blesses others. Or you may want to devote your life to public service, working in government to bring about policy change to help those who are poor, without housing, or battling addiction.

The truth is that your dreams, no matter how noble, can be tanked by your exterior life. And your exterior life, your words and actions, always betray what you really are on the inside.

The life of the messenger matters. Through every word, choice, and action, you're always telling your story.

A father went away on a business trip for several days, leaving his young family. He wanted to make sure his wife was cared for during his trip, so he called his oldest son to him, who was nine at the time, and said, "When I'm away, I want you to do what I would normally do around the house. Whatever you think I would do, you do that." The father had in mind cleaning up the kitchen, washing the dishes, taking out the garbage, and so on.

When he got home he asked his wife what his son had done. She said, "It was the strangest thing. Right after breakfast he drank a second cup of coffee, went to the living room, yelled at the dog, and read the newspaper for an hour."

No matter what positive things the father had done to help his wife and family, ultimately his exterior, negative example rested in the heart of the son. Many parents say, "Do as I say, not as I do." But actions speak louder than words. Don't be surprised if people judge your character based on what you actually do rather than on what you say. The genuine, authentic life is developed through careful attention and an interplay between what's within and how one lives it out.

The Quest for the Authentic Self

The temptation to dress up the exterior rather than focusing on the interior will likely be a challenge for you. Why? Because it's the easier path. With a little money and time, I can purchase clothes to give a certain impression, drive the right car, identify with the right causes, and say things that I know will please and even dazzle others. But let me tell you from experience, that's exhausting. It costs a lot more to perpetuate that kind of life because it never ends. Creating a false image of yourself is draining, and many people gravitate toward the authentic life (or at least want it more) because they can't perpetuate their false selves any longer.

Thomas Merton said,

> Every one of us is shadowed by an illusory person of false self . . . this is the person that I want myself to be but who cannot exist, because God— because Truth, Light—knows nothing about him. And to be unknown to God is altogether too much privacy. My false and private self is the one who wants to exist outside the reach of God's will and God's love— outside of reality and outside of life. And such a self cannot help but be an illusion.[4]

Magicians spend years cultivating illusions. They don't come easily, and they don't last. Eventually the scheme is revealed.

I've loved cars since I was a kid. Cars provide a kind of status symbol, and while some love BMW and Mercedes, the Jeep Wrangler was always the object of my pursuit. Jeeps represent an off-road, wilderness kind of life, and I dreamed of owning one and driving it around with mud splashed all over.

As soon as we could afford it, I bought a new Jeep. It was a beautiful, electric lime color. We lived in a rural setting at the time, and it was common for me to take it on dirt roads and through muddy ravines.

But it rarely got dirty. As much as I tried, I could never get the image that I longed for just right. The truth is that I spent a lot more time on the highway than on the back roads. People would actually comment on what a clean, shiny vehicle it was, subtly suggesting that I wasn't really a Jeep kind of guy.

Not long ago I learned about Spray-on Mud. Developed in Great Britain, Spray-on Mud was created "to give your friends, family, and neighbors the impression you've just come back from a day's shooting or fishing, anything but driving around town all day." For just $14.50, I could purchase liquid mud to spray on my bumpers, fenders, and doors to create the image that I was out in the woods all the time, fooling my neighbors and friends.[5]

We live in a spray-on authenticity culture. We want authenticity fast and we want it now, like we want everything else. But the authentic, genuine life doesn't come quickly, and it can't be purchased. The quest to overcome the illusory self with the true self is hard work, and it is costly, but not in dollars and cents.

Let me conclude this chapter with four suggestions for cultivating your authentic self.

First, *make self-understanding and self-care a priority.* It's not a waste of time to seek to get to know who you are; it's some of the most important work that you will ever do. It requires solitude, listening, and a willingness to face the truth of your strengths and weaknesses. This needs to happen in every stage of life. One of the most important questions you can ask is, *What am I most afraid of?* The things that create fear within us often lead to the invention of a false self. We are afraid that we will be rejected, wounded, or cast out, and that leads us to become something we are not.

We need silence, and not just every once in a while. Every week we need a time to be still and listen, take a walk, get fresh air, still our souls, and seek understanding. Books can help as long as we don't adopt ideas that fit others but not us. The care of a community is essential for self-understanding. Only in relationship with others can we fully see who we are.

Second, *get outside of yourself by serving others.* When we care for the needs of others, we not only see their humanity, brokenness, and pain but also recognize our own. Serving others is essential in the development of our souls. Reinhold Neibuhr said, "Man is the kind of animal who cannot merely live. If he lives at all he is bound to seek the realization of his true nature; and to his true nature belongs his fulfillment in the lives of others."[6]

Third, *have courage to speak what you see.* Ephesians 4:15 counsels, "Speak the truth in love." Speak out against injustice, speak out against racism, speak out against falsehood and the sham elements of our culture. You may see something that others can't, and now is the time for the truth to be spoken. Marianne Williamson said,

> Our deepest fear is not that we are inadequate. Our deepest fear is that we are powerful beyond measure. It is our light, not our darkness, that most frightens us. Your playing small does not serve the world. There is nothing enlightened about shrinking so that other people won't feel insecure around you. We are all meant to shine as children do. It's not just in some of us; it is in everyone. And as we let our own lights shine, we unconsciously give other people permission to do the same. As we are liberated from our own fear, our presence automatically liberates others.

An elementary school teacher was conducting a drawing class with a group of six-year-olds. At the back of the class sat a little girl who normally didn't pay much attention in school. But she loved the drawing class, and for more than twenty minutes she sat with her arms curled around the paper, totally absorbed in what she was doing. The teacher saw how focused she was on the project and asked her what she was drawing. Without looking up she said, "I'm drawing a picture of God." The teacher was surprised and said, "But nobody knows what God looks like." The girl said, "They will in a minute."[8]

We have to tell the world what we see, and we should do so in a way that is redemptive and compassionate, not strident and abrasive.

Fourth, *continually renounce the way of life that is all about image, perception, and self-promotion.* This isn't a one-time proclamation but an ongoing battle to push back against the dominant culture that promotes style over substance.

Our world needs genuine leaders who can show us a different way forward. We're waiting for you not only to be who you are but also to engage the quest of becoming your best self, inside and out.

Notes

1. e. e. cummings, "A Poet's Advice to Students" in *A Miscellany* (1958), edited by George James Firmage, 13.

2. Brené Brown, *The Gifts of Imperfection: Let Go of Who You Think You're Supposed to Be and Embrace Who You Are* (Center City MN: Hazelden Publishing, 2010).

3. Amy Morin, "3 Beliefs that Hold You Back from Living an Authentic Life," Huffpost (blog), June 7, 2016, huffingtonpost.com/amy-morin/3-beliefs-that-hold-you-b_b_10338702.html.

4. Thomas Merton, *New Seeds of Contemplation* (Boston: Shambhala, 2003) 36.

5. Check it out here: Jim Mateja, "Give Your SUV that Off-road Look—Just Apply Mud," *Chicago Tribune* (online), June 15, 2005, articles.chicagotribune.com/2005-06-15/business/0506150141_1_vanity-plate-spray-on-mud-neighbors.

6. Reinhold Neibuhr, *Major Works on Religion and Politics* (New York: Library of America, 2015) 366.

7. Marianne Williamson, *Return to Love: Reflections on the Principles of "A Course in Miracles"* (New York: HarperCollins, 1992) 190.

8. Ken Robinson, *The Element* (New York: Penguin Books, 2009) xi.

Chapter 4

Introspection

Deep within each person lies an inner stream of the soul.

My family of origin used to vacation with the Edwards family, whose children, Devron and Denise, were the same age as my brother and me. One summer in the Smoky Mountains we rented inner tubes and enjoyed a lazy river ride, with the exception of a brief rapid or two. Even in July, the frigid water could take your breath away. Devron, my brother, and I had moved through a rapid and stood in the shallows to one side of the river when Denise floated past us. She asked if it was very deep where she was, and we said no, knowing better. She hopped out and was immediately submerged. After a second she popped up, sputtering, shaking, and screaming at us to stop laughing.

Denise got a physical taste of the deep stream. But there's a metaphorical deep stream that most of us rarely touch, and it's evident in the way we show up in society. We're shallow, self-centered, and anxious. We find ourselves submerged in sound bites and the deluge of information overload. All the while, a consciousness of a potentially deeper, wilder, and ironically more peaceful life creeps at the edges, calling to us.

I long for the deep-stream life. How about you?

People are like rivers, most of which exist below the visible surface. We reveal only a small portion of who we are—our greatest strengths, most pressing fears—while the majority of ourselves works below the surface. We experience intense joy and overwhelming turmoil. Within our souls is an epic struggle for our thoughts, our time, our bodies, our very beings. And if we're not attentive to our souls, they will be diminished, co-opted and degraded over time.

The word *soul* brings to mind all kinds of ideas. A quick Internet search reveals hundreds of sites dedicated to the soul, from transcendental meditation to psychic development and dreams. According to the Bible, a person doesn't have a soul; a person *is* a soul. The Hebrew word for soul is *nephesh*, and it appears over 750 times in Scripture. It refers to the wholeness of someone, not individual parts. It is ultimately what is alive in us. The word *nephesh* actually means "throat." Think about that for a moment. The soul is the place of hunger, either experiencing satisfaction or dissatisfaction. We have a longing to be filled.

Our societal structures, then, from government agencies to church congregations, reflect the amalgamation and collaboration of souls. In some places, souls are nurtured, reverenced, and encouraged to thrive, but in other places, souls are diminished and starving for intimacy and peace.

While many people assume that the historic, orthodox Christian faith is monolithic, it actually is a wide, diverse, deep river that has been moving for more than two millennia, with a varied range of voices, experiences, and expressions. Faith in the shallows walks gingerly in religious clichés, superficial relationships, and stale rituals. Deep-stream faith asks hard questions, not shying away from doubt, pain, and failure. It's expansive and celebratory and authentic. Deep-stream faith seeks full immersion, which can occasionally astonish or jolt us.

I long for a deep-stream faith, for deep-stream church, and for deep-stream society. I believe there are many more people like me, perhaps with a small experience of immersion but who long to wade into deeper waters, believing that we can be deeper than what we are today.

But this won't happen without intentionality. If you dream of a deeper life experience, then start with yourself. You'll need an active inner life to go with your active external, community life. You'll need a sanctuary for your soul.

This is the part of us that is easiest to neglect. Busyness and anxiety dominate our days, actually pushing us away from contemplation and peace. In Thomas Kelly's classic *A Testament of Devotion*, we read, "Deep within us all there is an amazing inner sanctuary of the soul, a holy place, a Divine Center, a speaking Voice, to which we may continuously return. Eternity is at our hearts, pressing upon our time-torn lives, warming us with intimations of an astounding destiny, calling us home unto Itself."[1]

Mark Twain also spoke to the complexity of the inner life and the need to be attentive to what's happening within. "Life does not consist mainly— or even largely—of facts and happenings," he stated. "It consists mainly of the storm of thoughts that is forever blowing through one's head."[2]

Life and that "storm of thoughts" can be overwhelming. There's so much to take in, and our souls can feel overrun. It takes intentionality to quiet one's soul and experience things differently. While life seems to consist of everyday happenings and the ongoing succession of tasks, in truth it's more about connection and the inner workings of our souls in relationship. Our minds don't have to be a storm of thoughts, but instead can provide a quiet, foundational center from which we interact with the world. The truth is that people almost always know whether our inner lives are filled with calm and assurance or anxiety and restlessness.

Poet John O'Donohue said, "There is always an uncanny symmetry between the way you are inward with yourself and the way you are outward. And I feel that there is an evacuation of interiority going on in our times. And that we need to draw back inside ourselves and that we'll find immense resources there."[3] O'Donohue is right. We have immense resources from which to draw from that can sustain us. You'll need those kind of resources to be an effective community leader who doesn't burn out or become cynical.

Our culture desperately needs leaders who work from the inside out. Meister Eckhart said, "If your inner life is rich, the outer work will never be puny."[4] But it doesn't work the other way around. If your outer life is big, your inner life may shrivel. Eckhart also taught, "There is a place in the soul—there's a place in the soul that neither time, nor space, nor no created thing can touch."

The good news is that we are always closer to the deep stream than we think. The lack of depth and soul-attentiveness of our current political, spiritual, and social landscape may be giving way to a deeper, richer, and more soul-honoring way of life.

Thomas Merton said, "What can we gain by sailing to the moon if we cannot cross the abyss that separates us from ourselves?"[5] Crossing this abyss is the central challenge of the next generation. How can we discover ourselves? I believe our true selves are found not in new discovery but in uncovering and dusting off life-giving practices that nurture the care of our souls: silence and stillness.

Silence and Stillness

Paul Simon penned these words more than fifty years ago as a whispered polemic regarding the inability of many humans to be quiet:

> Hello darkness, my old friend,
> I've come to talk with you again
> Because a vision softly creeping
> Left its seeds while I was sleeping
> And the vision that was planted in my brain
> Still remains
> Within the sound of silence.[6]

Simon's words suggest a longing to enter into an intimate conversation with the darkness, expecting to hear and be heard. But the song continues as a warning against the dangers of technology and distractedness: *people talking without speaking . . . people hearing without listening.* When I recently heard this song again, my mind jumped to Twitter, where so many people are talking but few people are listening.

Under the noise, buzz, sirens, and pings of the world is a deep, almost frightening silence. We rush around and conduct business, acting as if we make the world turn, but in the meantime the earth produces foliage, the rains fall, and birds build nests. That's only a tiny fraction of the intricate, ever-changing life underneath our feet and around us. Most of it goes on in utter silence.

Why do we resist silence? Perhaps we are addicted to the noise, to the busyness, to ourselves. Perhaps we stay consumed with music, video, texts, and tweets to shield ourselves from that awful absence of sound where we are alone with our thoughts and forced to contemplate what is happening around us. Even so, I believe that more and more people yearn for stillness and peace. Those who move beyond yearning to the practical cultivation of a quiet heart discover that there are great benefits.

Here are three simple rewards of the practice of intentional silence and stillness:

First, *the quieter you become, the more you will hear.* You'll listen more when you don't feel the need to fill the void. You'll be a better listener for your friends or your spouse or your children. You'll experience more of this breathtaking world, noticing the sounds of the wind, of wildlife, of babies, of laughter.

Activist, poet, and farmer Wendell Berry lives enthusiastically with intense reverence for nature, calling people to simple living and good stewardship. He writes about a greater stillness this way: "I come into the peace of wild things. . . . I rest in the grace of the world, and am free."[7]

Second, *the quieter you become, the more you will speak rightly*. Dietrich Bonhoeffer said that right words come out of right silence, and right silence comes out of right words—an interplay between silence and word.

Third, *the quieter you become, the more you will open yourself to the mystery of the divine*. I heard a woman on the radio recently say, "I'm not religious, but when I sit in the silence of the desert, that's the closest I come to believing in God." In silence, surprisingly, many experience the intimate conversation that Paul Simon longed for, the encounter in the darkness.

Isaiah 30:15 says, "In returning and rest you shall be saved; in quietness and in trust shall be your strength" (ESV). Regardless of whether or not we attend to it, the silence remains. It waits like an old friend.

The book *Contact* by Carl Sagan (1985) tells the powerful story of a woman who is determined to discover if there is life beyond earth. She turns down a teaching position at a major university in order to spend time listening to radio signals from outer space. Everyone thinks she is crazy, wasting her time. She organizes a team of researchers and spends weeks, months, even years in the desert among large radio dishes, just listening, waiting, hoping to hear a signal. She is not sure what she will hear but believes that something is there, beyond her.

After several years, she has heard no signal. Her money has run out. All of her assistants have deserted her. She is at the end of her rope but remains determined. She heads out to listen again.

Everything is deathly quiet. Then, out of nowhere, she hears a distinctive signal. The crackled sound, like a heartbeat, grows louder and louder. She startles to attention. It's the message she has been waiting for. She has made contact.

What might you hear—either from within or perhaps in echoes from outside yourself—if you were to engage in the discipline of silence each week?

Mother Teresa, who practiced an active life of service, said in her book *In the Heart of the World*, "In the silence of the heart God speaks. If you face God in prayer and silence, God will speak to you. Then you will know that you are nothing. It is only when you realize your nothingness, your emptiness, that God can fill you with Himself. Souls of prayer are souls of great silence."[8]

In silence and stillness, we begin to understand a deeper way to live, a deeper kind of time.

Learning to Live in Deep Time

Early in my pastoral ministry I visited a prison to teach literacy. Each month on the second Tuesday evening, I arrived at Donaldson Correctional Facility in Jefferson County, Alabama, to tutor inmates. I have little recollection of what I said in those visits, but I have vivid memories of what people said to me. On one of the first visits I met BJ, a man who was described by others to be at one time one of the hardest, meanest criminals they had ever met. He was serving a life sentence for rape and double murder, and BJ knew that he would never get out.

But one weekend BJ decided to attend what was called a Kairos weekend at the prison, a ministry run by a local Methodist church. Something happened to BJ that weekend. He showed up for the free food, but by the end of the weekend something had radically changed in him. His hardness was replaced with gentleness, his violent spirit with a heart of peace. What made the difference?

In the Bible, there are two Greek words for *time*. There is *chronos*, which is chronological time, minutes, hours, days, and so on. It's time as one second after another in succession, and it's the way that most of us experience time.

But there is a second Greek word for time: *kairos*. *Kairos* is what Franciscan Richard Rohr calls *deep time*. *Kairos* is "when you have those moments where you say, 'Oh my god, this is it. I get it,' or, 'This is as perfect as it can be,' or, 'It doesn't get any better than this,' or, 'This moment is summing up the last five years of my life,' things like that where time comes to a fullness, and the dots connect, when we can learn how to more easily go back to those kind of moments or to live in that kind of space."[9]

Rohr teaches the importance of learning to live in deep time rather than *chronos* time. It's learning to live in the light of eternity rather than in the rush or urgency of the present moment. There's a way to live with a sense of rest and peace rather than being caught up in the anxieties of the present.

One way to practice deep time is by consistently asking the question, "Is this really going to matter on my deathbed?" When you come to the end of your life, what will truly have mattered? When I conduct funerals, the accomplishments of the person's life are usually mentioned, but those accomplishments never amount to the fullness of what makes a person's life significant. It's always the relationships and the way one made the lives of others better, even if only a few people, that hold weight in the final summation. It's the way the person learned to live at peace.

You can learn to live in *kairos* even as you experience the march of *chronos*. And by the way, if you haven't noticed, *chronos* moves pretty fast. The faster you learn to settle your mind and heart in deep time, *sub specie aeternitatis*—"in the light of eternity" —the more you'll be able to focus on the things that matter most.

Hope for the Overwhelmed

My mother made me join the swim team each summer during my elementary school years. Some kids love to swim, but not me. It felt like torture rolling out of bed at 6 a.m. on summer days and jumping in freezing cold water for the sixteen-lap warmup.

I never was a good swimmer, but one day I was especially struggling. Around lap twelve I couldn't go any farther. I remember the feeling of panic as my arms flailed and my lungs took in a gulp of water. The edges of consciousness blurred as I sank to the bottom.

Fortunately, someone jumped in to save me. But I'll never forget that feeling of utter helplessness.

There are moments when I feel like that kid again, and I know you do, too. Sometimes I long for a deeper immersion, but sometimes I feel the need for deliverance from circumstances that pose a threat to my soul. I meet people all the time who say that they feel like they're in over their heads. "I'm drowning," they say, "just trying to keep my head above water." The combination of hyper-busy schedules with no margins, excessive worry, and unexpected crises can leave one feeling fretful and in despair.

National Public Radio (NPR) conducted a study on stress in America and found that 49 percent of respondents said they had experienced a serious stressful event in the last year. Most of the events were health related (due to an illness or the death of a loved one), but respondents also cited things like too many responsibilities, financial problems, and work problems.

An estimated 40 million American adults suffer from anxiety disorders. About one-third of those who suffer receive treatment. In 2011, 11 percent of middle-aged women (ages 45–64) were on some kind of anti-anxiety drug, nearly twice as many as men. But men generally have a harder time asking for help or taking some kind of medication. A few months ago I spoke to a man in our congregation who for the first time in his life was having anxiety attacks. His heart rate would race, his chest would hurt, he would feel like he was going to pass out; after several attacks and doctors finding nothing else wrong with him, they diagnosed him as having anxiety attacks.

NPR also asked how people responded to stress: 70 percent said that they sleep less than usual when stressed; 43 percent exercise or play sports less than usual; and 41 percent reported they usually attend a religious service and pray more. That's interesting because it suggests that a lot of people show up to church stressed and needing some relief, but many churches actually give them more to do and put more burdens on them.[10]

Jesus said, "Peace I leave with you; my peace I give to you. Not as the world gives do I give to you. Let not your hearts be troubled, neither let them be afraid" (John 14:27, ESV). We shouldn't think that Jesus is some kind of genie in a bottle, summoned to give us peace whenever we want it. Instead, Jesus taught us the kind of life that will bring peace. It won't protect us from chaos and disruption, but it will not ultimately be shaken.

How can you experience that kind of life?

First, *build on something solid.* Like a home, every life needs a foundation. Jesus said, "Everyone then who hears these words of mine and does them will be like a wise man who built his house on the rock" (Matt 7:24, ESV). When we hear his words and put them into practice, we make a life of peace for ourselves. Refusing to worry, ceasing from judging others, telling the truth (all of these are found in the Sermon on the Mount) are actions that naturally incline toward a life of peace within and with one's neighbor.

Second, *be a peacemaker.* "Blessed are the peacemakers," Jesus said, "for they shall be called children of God" (Matt 5:9, ESV). Be a "maker" (craftsman, artist, creator) of peace in your family, work, and community (even among your enemies).

Third, *pray in all things.* This is one of the most challenging practices of the life of faith, but the more you practice, the easier it becomes. Paul wrote, "in everything by prayer and supplication with thanksgiving, let your requests be made known to God" (Phil 4:6, ESV). The accompanying promise is that God's peace will guard our hearts and minds.

The hardest thing to believe is that someone is nearby to jump in when we hit bottom, but it is true. There is hope for the overwhelmed. Whatever you want to accomplish in your life, in public policy, with religious life, in the education of others, or in any other field, you'll need a sanctuary for your soul. You'll need a robust inner life to balance your active external life.

Notes

1. Thomas R. Kelly, *A Testament of Devotion* (1941; repr., New York: Harper Collins, 1996) 1.

2. Mark Twain, *Autobiography of Mark Twain: Volume 1*, ed. Harriet Elinor Smith (Berkeley: University of California Press, 2010) 256.

3. John O'Donohue, quoted in the On Being podcast transcript, August 6, 2015, onbeing.org/programs/john-odonohue-the-inner-landscape-of-beauty/.

4. As quoted by Pico Ayer in the On Being podcast transcript, May 5, 2016, onbeing.org/programs/krista-tippett-the-mystery-and-art-of-living/.

5. Thomas Merton, *The Wisdom of the Desert* (New York: New Directions, 1960) 11.

6. Paul Simon, "Sound of Silence," *Wednesday Morning, 3 A.M.*, Columbia Records, 1964.

7. First published in *Openings: Poems* (1968).

8. Mother Teresa, *In the Heart of the World* (New World Library, 1997).

9. Richard Rohr, quoted in *On Being* podcast (transcript), April 13, 2017, onbeing.org/programs/richard-rohr-living-in-deep-time/.

10. Scott Hensley and Alyson Hurt, "Stressed Out: Americans Tell Us about Stress in Their Lives," NPR (online transcript from radio program), July 7, 2014, npr.org/sections/health-shots/2014/07/07/327322187/stressed-out-americans-tell-us-about-stress-in-their-lives.

Chapter 5

Vulnerability

Love always comes with a risk.

Born in Joplin, Mississippi, Langston Hughes was among the greatest poets of the early twentieth century. Hughes wrote books, poems, and novels while also serving his community as a social activist in a time of intense racism. His grandmother had been a slave, sharing stories with him about the hardness of slavery days. But Hughes did not know if America would ever get any better. At the age of twenty-one, he wrote a poem called "Mother to Son," perhaps based on something that his mother spoke to him:

Well, son, I'll tell you:
Life for me ain't been no crystal stair.
It's had tacks in it,
And splinters,
And boards torn up,
And places with no carpet on the floor—
Bare.
But all the time
I'se been a-climbin' on,
And reachin' landings,
And turnin' corners,
And sometimes goin' in the dark
Where there ain't been no light.

So boy, don't you turn back.
Don't you set down on the steps
'Cause you finds it's kinder hard.
Don't you fall down now—
For I'se still goin', honey,
I'se still climbin',
And life for me ain't been no crystal stair.[1]

The next generation is a hopeful generation. That's good, because many people in earlier generations would tell you that life is no crystal stair. It can be dangerous and dark, and while there are successes to enjoy and places of rest, you can't turn back and you can't give up. You've got to keep climbing in this life. You can't sit down just because it's hard.

As millennials, you're entering a world where there has been much technological and scientific progress leading to unprecedented connectedness. But for all of our advancements, it seems that we have yet to grasp what it means to be human and how to love our neighbors. With all the progress in the fields of technology, science, medicine, and social and psychological understanding, still the challenges of income inequality, mass incarceration, food insecurity (a regular circumstance of not having enough food to thrive), and racism in our neighborhoods and workplaces persist. Our politics are a mess. Churches are struggling. Just about everyone you meet is carrying a heavy load.

Even though life may be hard, you have to keep climbing. You have to keep dreaming. In a 1961 commencement address at Lincoln University, Martin Luther King Jr. spoke about "The American Dream": "America is essentially a dream, a dream as yet unfulfilled." Dreamers know that some dreams will be unfulfilled in their lifetime or even shattered. In fact, King preached sermons titled "Unfulfilled Dreams" and "Shattered Dreams." He said, "Few of us live to see our fondest hopes fulfilled." But that didn't stop him from dreaming. He still had the courage to dream and to keep climbing, knowing that not all dreams come true and that the pursuit of a dream is not a crystal stair.

In such a climate, it would be easy to withdraw, to avoid sharing who you are and being the best self for your own good and the good of others. And that is exactly what many people do. The last thing they want to be is vulnerable, because that is precisely how they feel a good bit of the time: vulnerable, at-risk, unprotected, emotionally exposed.

Vulnerability is openness to the possibility of being wounded. It's easy to understand why people do not want to be vulnerable. But the word "vulnerable" is a strange word. It's not clear whether it speaks to certain harm with no purpose or to harm that may be chosen so that something else can be gained. A child is vulnerable if that child climbs a tree, opening the possibility of physical harm, but that doesn't keep the child from climbing the tree for the adventure and view. Someone who bravely steps into the political realm, risking financial and emotional harm, could do so with eyes wide open, knowing that failure may be imminent.

M. Scott Peck wrote in his book *A Different Drum,*

> There is no way that we can live a rich life unless we are willing to suffer repeatedly, experiencing depression and despair, fear and anxiety, grief and sadness, anger and the agony of forgiving, confusion and doubt, criticism and rejection. A life lacking these emotional upheavals will not only be useless to ourselves, it will be useless to others. We cannot heal without being willing to be hurt.[2]

Our world needs healing. I need healing, and so do you. Life is no crystal stair, and many stop climbing because it's too hard. The cost seems too high. But Jesus taught that the only way to be healed—the only way to salvation—is through vulnerability. He took his place among the broken, the outcasts, those who were infected. He spent his time among the most vulnerable in society. And then he displayed the ultimate vulnerability by being led to the cross "like a lamb to the slaughter" (Isa 53:7, NIV). We think that the path to healing must go through the overcoming and avoidance of weakness, the will to power over those who oppose us, even when we believe that we're on the side of the angels. But Jesus demonstrated a greater power that is available to every human: the power that comes through a vulnerable and open posture, being willing to be wounded for the healing of the world.

Vulnerability Is Strength

What happens when we make ourselves vulnerable?

I was sitting at my daughter's lacrosse game, half watching and half checking my phone for sports scores and headlines. Emily's team was crushing the other team (that was rare!) and the parents were bored. To my right, I heard two African American women talking about one of the daughters on the field and the suffering she had endured. I began to listen.

The daughter had grown up gregarious, with no fear and always happy, but four years beforehand, in the fourth grade, she had been bullied by two white kids at school and called racial slurs. It damaged her. She became quiet and fearful. She began to struggle with her grades. The moms were talking about how she was doing better now, how her family had home-schooled her for a while, and that now she was back in a different public school.

I wanted to hear more, so I stood up and came closer to them. At first it was awkward. I felt like I had stumbled into a conversation that was not intended for someone like me. But I said, "I couldn't help but hear what you're talking about, and I just wanted to listen." After a moment, the mom let her guard down and kept talking. The more I heard, the more I felt her pain and wanted to express a measure of empathy.

I can't fix what happened to her daughter, but I can listen and suspend judgment for a while. If we can learn to listen to each other and empathize, we may be able to find some ways to do things differently and heal the wounds of the past.

To be clear, I'm not saying that this woman's daughter should have to endure suffering, that somehow she should gladly endure pain and weakness in the name of vulnerability. What I am saying is that only through openness and truth-telling can we overcome problems of racism, bigotry, inequality, and unfairness. Only then can healing begin and a new way be forged.

It's tough to admit that *this* is what happened to me . . . to my friend . . . to my spouse . . . to my child. It's hard to say that we have been hurt and bullied or that we feel lost and scared and uncertain of the future. But that mother's vulnerability, while perhaps feeling like weakness, was actually strength.

The effect of vulnerability on others is almost always disarming. While it's possible to elicit a reaction where someone can be wounded even further, most often vulnerability leads someone to say, "How can I help?" When a person shares a deep wound with us, we feel like we have been invited into a holy place in their lives, one not shared with everyone. We are able to respond, "I have been wounded, too."

The opposite is also true. When people put up their defenses all the time, ready for battle, then, as Peck said, "personal relationships become nothing more than that of two empty tanks bumping against each other in the night."[3] This dynamic plays out on the personal level as well as in national and international relations. Invulnerability is the norm. But what if we were to begin to personally and corporately practice a posture not of foolish vulnerability, one that blindly ignores threats or the dangerous tendencies of criminal and terrorist organizations, but of hopeful vulnerability that allows leaders of goodwill to work together out of our common woundedness and need?

As mentioned in the introduction, in his sermon "Love Your Enemies," Martin Luther King Jr. described a night he rode with his brother from Atlanta to Chattanooga, Tennessee. As his brother drove, for some reason the drivers on the opposite side of the road weren't dimming their lights. King recalls how his brother A. D. looked over at him and, in a tone of anger, said, "I know what I'm going to do. The next car that comes along here and refuses to dim the lights, I'm going to fail to dim mine." He wanted to give them what he was being given, to pay them back for their wrongdoing. Martin King looked at him quickly and said, "Oh no, don't do that. There'd be too much light on this highway, and it will end up in mutual destruction for all. Somebody's got to have some sense on this highway."

We might say that this is the heart of the trouble in our world. We believe that the only way to be victorious is to be the strongest, most intimidating, or most resolute in demanding to be seen and heard. Too few people have sense enough to dim the lights. King added these beautiful words:

> If I hit you and you hit me and I hit you back and you hit me back and so on, you see, that goes on ad infinitum. It just never ends. Somewhere, somebody must have a little sense, and that's the strong person. The strong person is the person who can cut off the chain of hate, the chain of evil. And that is the tragedy of hate, that it doesn't cut it off. It only intensifies the existence of hate and evil in the universe. Somebody must have religion enough and morality enough to cut it off and inject within the very structure of the universe that strong and powerful element of love.[4]

At its heart, vulnerability is about the possibility of love. And love always comes with a risk. But it's also true that love is the strongest force in the world, worth every risk.

Henri Nouwen said, "The greatest gift we can give each other is our own woundedness."[5] When we admit our hurts and our mistakes, our failures as well as our successes, we give a rare and precious gift that strengthens us and others along the way.

Just Relationships

Vulnerability also opens us to being deeply connected to people and caring for them in more than a passing way. The word "justice" occurs 200 times in the Old Testament, and it holds the idea that everyone is treated with the same fairness, no matter their skin color or position in society. It also means giving people their due. Every person is created in the *imago dei*, the image of God. A life of justice means that your relationships will extend to some people who are different from you because you believe that they should be afforded the same worth and dignity that you have. Biblical justice is rooted not in an idea of the inherent worth of every person but in relationship to the God of justice. If God is a God of justice, showing no partiality and caring for everyone equally, then our relationships need to reflect the same love and tender care that God has for all people.

For those who are about justice, vulnerability is an essential quality. Every relationship becomes sacred as people have the desire to be connected to all through fairness and equal concern. Who in your life would you call the "most vulnerable," and what place do they have at your table, if any? Who is being exploited, or treated as someone as less than human? Who is being ignored? Who in your life have you written off? Do you spend all your energy on yourself and on the relationships that benefit only you?

I love this description from Job 29:12-16:

> I delivered the poor who cried for help, and the fatherless who had none to help him. The blessing of him who was about to perish came upon me, and I caused the widow's heart to sing for joy. I put on righteousness, and it clothed me; my justice was like a robe and a turban. I was eyes to the blind and feet to the lame. I was a father to the needy, and I searched out the cause of him whom I did not know. (ESV)

The Bible frequently references groups of people who are often called the "quartet of the vulnerable": widows, orphans, foreigners, and the poor. These four groups had no social power. They lived at subsistence level and were often only days from starvation if there was any famine, invasion, or even minor social unrest. Today, this quartet would be expanded to include the refugee, the homeless, and many single parents and elderly people. The justness of a society, according to the Bible, is evaluated by how it treats these groups.

If we're going to have a more just, reconciled society, we need to care for those who are most vulnerable. Just relationships have two important qualities: generosity and empathy.

Generosity is possible because most of us have more than enough. We can become convinced of the opposite, however: that we need to protect what we have, that nothing is guaranteed, and that people are only out to take advantage of us. Often we build walls between ourselves and others due to our fear that something will be taken from us or that we won't have enough. A generous spirit counters these fears. Those who believe that they have been blessed to be a blessing, rather than blessed only to have more for themselves, are among the happiest people in our society.

Empathy is the ability to understand and relate to one another. It involves listening more than talking and a willingness to hear someone else's story without passing judgment. Rather than a stiff arm, empathy is an embrace. I really believe that what we need in this moment is not more judgment, more yelling past one another, or more finger pointing; what we need is more listening and embracing and being present in one another's lives.

I was in Gatlinburg, Tennessee, some years ago with a group of youth, and several of us were walking down the street, past candy and T-shirt shops and attractions. One lady was trying to sell people vacations. We were already on vacation, but she was trying to sell the next vacation, staying at this or that resort. As people walked by, she harassed them. She stopped them, talking fast; she wouldn't let people move past her on the sidewalk. I was annoyed and tried to ignore her. But just ahead of us was a family with a little girl. As this lady harassed the girl's family and wouldn't let them go, the little girl suddenly reached out and embraced the woman. The woman was speechless and embraced the little girl back, and I could see tears welling up in the woman's eyes.

I don't believe we have the luxury of ignoring one another anymore. To change the dynamic in a relationship, to enter into the pain of others, to move into the sorrow of others and even the rejoicing of others, we need to stop holding people at arm's length.

Don't Be Afraid

The feeling of vulnerability is acute in our society, but perhaps especially in the millennial generation. Somehow, those who have the most resources and the best opportunities still feel exposed and unable to cope with

the complexities of life. R. R. Reno calls this feeling "a pervasive disqui-
etude" that is transforming our culture and politics. Citing such factors as
increasing competitiveness in American institutions, insecurity regarding
future job prospects, the persistence of relational tension, falseness in social
media interactions, and unsettled questions about whether one should
get married or have children, Reno suggests that young adults have good
reason to wonder what a happy and productive life really looks like. For
example, your boss is your friend on Facebook and wears a T-shirt, but he
has the ability to fire you.[6] That's a tough tension to balance.

The feeling of impermanence is striking. Reno continues,

> To a certain extent, we're aware of this problem, and we adopt therapeutic
> strategies of affirmation, which means non-judgmentalism and a stren-
> uous rhetoric of inclusion. Everybody has the right to a life journey of his
> own choosing. Everyone's personal choices are to be respected. The idea
> here is to forestall feelings of vulnerability by preventing harsh, hurtful
> encounters.

In other words, a generation that values tolerance and personal choice may
often be avoiding hard conversations and pain more than they think. It's no
wonder that many young people value feeling "safe" as a top priority. They
just don't feel safe most days.

To lead in such a context, the next generation will need to face their
fears. Fear constantly asks, "What if?" What if I can't find a job? What if my
marriage can't survive? What if I can't overcome my depression? What if I
can't figure out what to do with my life? What if I never find someone to
love and to share a life with me? It's helpful to remember that the challenges
of the next generation are similar to the challenges that every generation
faces: discovering purpose, moving through uncertainty, finding love and
security. The volume of information consumption may be greater and cause
a heightened sense of uncertainty, but the questions have always existed.

I'd like to propose two simple tools for dealing with such fears:
intentional relationships and conversation. Specifically, we need greater
conversation up the chain of generations. The millennial generation is
often unmoored from deep relationships across generational lines. Many
young people have come into my life in search of a mentor or just an older
friend who can help them navigate the uncertainties of change.

With more conversation and storytelling, the next generation will learn
from the mature adults in our society that there have been and will always

be "what ifs." There have always been and will always be threats and pain, and without hope it's easy to fall into a mindset of distrust and fear. What we need is someone in our lives who has gone before us who can sit with us and, even if they can't solve all of our problems, at least offer this assurance: "It's going to be okay."

One of the most powerful questions we can ask ourselves is, "What would I do if I weren't afraid?"

When we deal with "what ifs" of fear, we can begin to entertain the "what ifs" of a better world. What if poverty in America could be abolished in our lifetime? What if the rising tide of mental illness were pushed back? What if we could look past skin color and see the need, brokenness, and weakness of a fellow human being?

I began this chapter with Langston Hughes, and that's where I'll end. In "I Dream a World," he offers a picture of justice and joy and security yet to be realized. (Hughes uses the word "man" to mean all humanity.)

I dream a world where man
No other man will scorn,
Where love will bless the earth
And peace its paths adorn. . . .[7]

Yes, we live in a vulnerable world. Life is no crystal stair. But the path upward is through vulnerability. That's how we'll climb, and that's how we'll get there, together.

Notes

1. Langston Hughes, "Mother to Son," transcript viewed June 15, 2017, onbeing.org/program/john-lewis-the-art-discipline-of-nonviolence/transcript/5156.

2. M. Scott Peck, A Different Drum (New York: Touchstone; Simon and Schuster, 1987) 226.

3. Ibid., 228.

4. Martin Luther King, Jr., "Love Your Enemies," sermon delivered at Dexter King Memorial Church, Montgomery AL, November 17, 1957, kingencyclopedia.stanford.edu/encyclopedia/documentsentry/doc_loving_your_enemies/.

5. Henri Nouwen, The Wounded Healer (Garden City: Doubleday 1972).

6. R. R. Reno, "Politics of Vulnerability," First Things website, October 2016, firstthings.com/article/2016/10/politics-of-vulnerability.

7. Langston Hughes, "I Dream a World," available at langston-hughes.weebly.com/poem.html.

Chapter 6

Reverence

Every story—every life—matters.

Every human life is sacred. Every person deserves to be heard and honored with respect assigned to their life experience. Each life has a place in the world.

But we live in an age that celebrates condemnation, criticism, scorn, disdain, and disrespect. It's the opposite of honor and awe at the sacred life of another. We see this in our politics and on social media. There's little sense of the sacred. There's rarely reverence for oneself, for others, or for the great stories that bind us together.

Thus, we need more reverence in our collective life. There have been examples of great women and men, even ages of American life, with a sense of reverence and awe for our political interactions and an appreciation for the differences we may hold. We might call our current age a valley in American life, but we have glimpsed the mountaintop. There have been eras of greater cooperation. There have been moments that define the essence of America, where we have caught a vision for what our better selves can be.

Albert Schweitzer was once referred to as the most famous of any person alive. That's not common for a missionary. He challenged millions of people to realize a simple but profound revelation: how rich human life can be. He called people to an appreciation and even reverence for the beauty of nature. But he especially called for reverence of each person as a soul. "No one can give a definition of the soul," he said. "But we know what it feels like. The soul is the sense of something higher than ourselves, something that stirs in us thoughts, hopes, and aspirations which go out to the world of goodness, truth and beauty. The soul is a burning desire to breathe in this world of light and never to lose it—to remain children of light."[1]

Born on January 14, 1875, Schweitzer grew up to study music, philosophy, and theology. He began his career as pastor of a small church between 1900 and 1905 in Strasbourg, Germany. But in 1905, he made a radical change and decided to devote the rest of his life to serving people in equatorial Africa through medical care. He reentered the university to receive a physician's degree, then traveled to Africa and eventually established the Albert Schweitzer Hospital in Lambaréné, now in Gabon, west central Africa (then French Equatorial Africa).

During a 200-kilometer steamboat journey in Africa in 1915, Schweitzer was inspired with a new concept, what he would call *the reverence for life*. This phrase would become for Schweitzer a kind of philosophy of life that involved not only humans but all of creation. "As far back as I can remember," he said, "I was saddened by the amount of misery I saw in the world around me." He devoted nearly fifty years of his life to caring for health needs while also writing books on religion, music, and art.

Our current political atmosphere calls attention to failures and challenges, such as schools in crisis, what has been called the school-to-prison pipeline, and the rise in terrorism. There's plenty of blame to go around. We speak easily to *what* our problems are, but we don't often speak to *why* these problems are so egregious.

The *why* of these problems deals with real people with real experiences. These are children of God who are, as our Declaration of Independence states, "endowed by their Creator with certain unalienable Rights, that among these are Life, Liberty and the pursuit of Happiness." There is a reverence in those words that propels an economic and political argument to the realm of the sacred.

Paul Woodruff, author of *Reverence: Renewing a Forgotten Virtue*, says that reverence is "the capacity for awe in the face of the transcendent." By "transcendent," he means "whatever humans did not create: God, justice, the truth, nature, beauty."[2]

Woodruff writes that reverence is "the well-developed capacity to have feelings of awe, respect, and shame when these are the right feelings to have."[3]

The next generation of American leaders will need the virtue of reverence to lead us. They'll need an appreciation for the sacred and a willingness to value the essential humanity of others. Reverence for themselves, for others, and for the grand narrative of America is not optional; it is essential.

Reverence for Others

In the novel *All the Light We Cannot See* by Anthony Doerr, one of the characters repeats this mantra: *Open your eyes and see what you can with them before they close forever.*

I feel like my eyes were opened recently, among all places, while waiting with my daughter to visit the orthodontist. It was such a routine life moment that I almost missed what was happening around me.

On a loud flat-screen TV, the grieving mothers of Trayvon Martin, Eric Garner, Tamir Rice, Sandra Bland, and Michael Brown appeared together on a show to talk about race in America.

At first I thought, *Who are these women?* and *Why is everyone crying?*—including the audience—but it wasn't long before I also felt tears rising. Each mother had experienced the worst this life can give: the death of a child.

Martin was a seventeen-year-old African American killed by George Zimmerman in Sanford, Florida, on February 26, 2012. Garner, an older African-American male, died on July 17, 2014, on Staten Island, New York City, by means of a police chokehold that medical examiners classified as a homicide. The officer was not indicted, and the Garner family was awarded a $5.9 million settlement in July 2015. Twelve-year-old Rice was shot by police on November 22, 2014, after reports came in "of a male black sitting on a swing and pointing a gun at people" in a city park. It turned out to be an Airsoft gun. Bland was arrested on July 10, 2015, during a traffic stop and was later found hanged in a Texas jail cell. Initially ruled as a suicide, Bland's death was later investigated as a murder. The officer involved was indicted for perjury and fired. The family settled a wrongful death suit for nearly $2 million, and charges against the officer were later dropped in return for his leaving law enforcement. Brown was killed in Ferguson, Missouri, on August 9, 2014, after an altercation with police. An investigation concluded the officer shot in self-defense.

There are significant details not represented in the brief descriptions of these deaths, including the perspectives of law enforcement. But to see these five grieving mothers sit together, comfort one another, tell their stories, and talk about their children was both sorrowful and deeply moving. It demonstrated to me not only their personal loss but also profound community loss and outrage.

I felt a bit like scales were falling off my eyes, and I could see their pain, better understand the stories of my neighbors, and more clearly recognize our need as a nation to address our problem with race.

We have a problem with race. Maybe we're ashamed to talk about it because we haven't come as far as we wanted, or maybe we're ashamed that so many people have favored re-segregation and de-integration in their personal choices throughout so many decades since the civil rights struggles of the 1950s and 1960s.

We haven't listened closely enough when our African-American brothers and sisters have kept saying *there is still a problem. There is still a problem. There is still a problem.*

We have spoken for too long of the *white community* and the *black community* and the *Latino community* rather than talking about *our community* and the common dreams and needs. We have gotten used to segregated neighborhoods and re-segregated schools and, most to our shame, we have sanctified in our churches the reasoning that different races can't come together.

I am using *we* as the pronoun, but I really mean *I.* It does no good to describe problems in general unless I get down to the specific, to my personal responsibility for my community.

Those grieving mothers are my neighbors. Those children are my children, too. We are all part of a human family and an American family. We are all part of an intricate web, young and old, police officers and everyday citizens, all of us wanting the same things: safe neighborhoods; good education for our children; compassionate care for the elderly; life, liberty, and happiness.

It was like a pleading from those five weeping women: *open your eyes and see.*

What do you see? What are the needs of the people around you? Start there. Begin to listen to their stories and value their essential dignity and right to be heard.

Their Story Is My Story

Above my desk hangs a photo of my grandfather at two years old. He's standing in front of the shotgun house where he was born in Excel,

Alabama, his grandmother to his right and his three older brothers to his left. My grandfather's mother died young, leaving the four boys to be raised by their grandmother. He would grow up, meet my grandmother, open a grocery store, raise three children, and do a thousand other things that make up a life before passing away on July 9, 1974. I didn't know him well—I was four when he died—but even so, his story is my story. The photo reminds me that we are still connected, by DNA and shared history, by places and memories and faith and family.

But who I am extends beyond my family ties. Countless others have affected my life, and my life has affected countless others' lives. My coworkers, close friends, neighbors, and other people I see around Oak Cliff now play a daily role in shaping my story, and my story shapes theirs.

Speaking to a student group in 1964, Martin Luther King, Jr., said,

> . . . all life is interrelated, and in a real sense we are all courting an inescapable network of mutuality, tied in a single garment of destiny. Whatever affects one directly, affects all indirectly. For some strange reason, I can never be what I ought to be until you are what you ought to be. And you can never be what you ought to be until I am what I ought to be.[4]

Mutuality suggests deeply linked relationships and respect, but it also means responsibility for one another. It's the recognition that we need one another.

I live now in an area of Dallas called Oak Cliff. We see this principle of mutuality more fully at work than in other parts of the city. We value diversity, welcome different cultural expressions, and generally want to help and care for one another. But we have a long way to go. We struggle to cross racial, ethnic, economic, and lifestyle lines. We struggle even to cross the street. Neighbors often don't know the people nearest to them. We fail to recognize how much we need one another, and, consequently, we don't make the effort to cultivate relationships that go deeper than the surface.

What can we do? We can pursue new relationships and deepen existing relationships. We can slow down long enough to notice those who seem isolated or hurt and assume a courageous responsibility for helping them. We can give a few hours a month for the betterment of our neighborhoods.

In a word, we can show a little reverence for the stories of others. Only together can we wrestle with, discover, and celebrate the answers to life's biggest questions. Why are we here? What does it mean to be human with respect to other creatures and the environment? What does a just and peaceful city look like? What is the meaning of this story in which we all play a part?

Barack Obama said that when he began his career as a community organizer, the man who hired him told him that

> the thing that brings people together to have the courage to take action on behalf of their lives is not just that they care about the same issue, it's that they have shared stories. And he told me that if you learn how to listen to people's stories and can find what's sacred in other people's stories, then you'll be able to forge a relationship that lasts.[5]

Reverence for Oneself and the World

In his book *Rediscovering Reverence*, Ralph Heintzman argues that "reverence is the posture we adopt when we become conscious of our place in a larger order we did not create and do not control, about which we have little, if any free choice. You can't feel reverence for what you yourself create, control and understand."[6]

Those who have no reverence for themselves, or for a higher ideal, rarely hold true reverence for others. I believe we need to cultivate an appreciation for ourselves as well as for the broader narrative of the world we share and the society we have a part in creating.

First, you need a sense of reverence for yourself. Love yourself, just as you are, with your faults, beauty, and wonder. Learn to quiet the voices of negativity and defeat, voices that may shame you or push you down. How many leaders have made a mess of their communities because they were seeking self-aggrandizement, the approval of the crowd, or the need for power to fill a deep void in their lives?

Each life is mysterious, including yours. You are a *political* being, part of a collective. Every time you make a banking transaction, pay taxes, drive a car, or take part in an organization, it's always part of a system of relationships, authority, and shared responsibility. The word *polis* simply means city. There's no escaping a political life. But you are also a *spiritual* being. All that is within you—your physical, emotional and mental self—combines in such a way that suggests there is something unique and worthy of reverence.

In *Conjectures of a Guilty Bystander*, the Catholic monk and activist Thomas Merton wrote,

At the center of our being is a point of nothingness which is untouched by sin and by illusion, a point of pure truth, a point or spark which belongs entirely to God, which is never at our disposal, from which God disposes of our lives, which is inaccessible to the fantasies of our own mind or the brutalities of our own will. This little point of nothingness and of absolute poverty is the pure glory of God in us. It is so to speak [God's] name written in us, as our poverty, as our indigence, as our dependence, as our sonship [and daughtership]. It is like a pure diamond, blazing with the invisible light of heaven. It is in everybody, and if we could see it we would see these billions of points of light coming together in the face and blaze of a sun that would make all the darkness and cruelty of life vanish completely . . . . I have no program for this seeing. It is only given. But the gate of heaven is everywhere.[7]

Whatever one's faith, belief, or worldview, almost all of us believe in the value of other human beings and the need to show them honor. We can't do that unless we first extend that perspective to ourselves.

Second, you need a reverence for the larger world. A few years ago, on the Fourth of July, I sat in the high seats of the Cotton Bowl watching Dallas's fireworks with a few thousand others and marveling at the experience. How often does one sit with strangers, staring up and joining in the chorus of "ahh!" each time a particularly stunning array of color splits the sky?

You may think it strange, but the "ahh!" moment captures something of the heart of reverence. We yearn for the "ahh!" experience, but it requires attentiveness. It gives attention to the mystery, often in dedicated space and for dedicated time. As in other spheres of life, good habits lead to meaningful moments. We celebrate the victory moment for Olympic athletes, but what we admire is the devotion and attention—the practice—given to a singular pursuit. Similarly, those who experience transcendence practice giving attention.

The poet Mary Oliver wrote, "The dream of my life is to lie down by a slow river / And stare at the light of the trees— / To learn something by being nothing / A little while but the rich / Lens of attention."[8] In a world of endless distraction, developing a lens of simple attention can be a gateway to the deeper life.

Reverence of the larger world also requires vulnerability. It's about having your heart cracked open and allowing your mind to dance on dreams that the grind of life crowds out. This means, of course, that reverence is also about connection. Only through vulnerability can real connection become reality.

Reverence for the American Story

My friend Daniel recently became a United States citizen. It was a big moment for him and his family as he took an oath of allegiance with many other new citizens. His journey to reach this point was long. It took several years and lots of money. He had to fill out many forms, be interviewed, and learn American history before he could take his oath. These are things I have never had to do as a US citizen. I was born here and educated in American schools, so it's kind of a given that I would stand and say the pledge, learn US history, and so on. But I've never been required to take an oath, and, like many adults, I would struggle with facts about presidents and our political system and important historical moments.

Why would Daniel and his family come here?

The truth is that the American narrative is compelling, and many people choose it. At the very least, it's likely to be a better choice economically, socially, and politically than wherever someone may came from. The American narrative is that if someone is willing to work hard and sacrifice, then there are great possibilities for success. Through a culture that celebrates freedom, access to education, fair economic practices, and public infrastructure, one can make a better life.

So, to conclude this chapter, I want to call us to a sense of reverence for our collective story, the American story. Without making our country an idol, we must cultivate a sense of reverence for the American narrative, one that speaks to the best of our intentions and what we can accomplish together.

We share a common, if imperfect, story together. We make the story that will be told one day to our children and grandchildren.

In *Moyers on Democracy*, Bill Moyers said,

Democracy in America is a series of narrow escapes, and we may be running out of luck. The reigning presumption about the American experience . . . is grounded in the idea of progress, the conviction that the present is "better" than the past and the future will bring even more improvement. For all of its shortcomings, we keep telling ourselves, "The system works." Now all bets are off. We have fallen under the spell of money, faction, and fear, and the great American experience in creating a different future together has been subjugated to individual cunning in the pursuit of wealth and power—and to the claims of empire, with its ravenous demands and stuporous distractions.[9]

How can we start to find our way back, or, if you prefer, to forge a better future, that allows us to move beyond fear and faction? How can we rediscover a collective vision of helping one another to succeed, loving our neighbor, and becoming the people that we know we can be?

Perhaps we can begin with reverence. Reverence is possible when we clearly know the distance between an ideal we have and our ability to reach that ideal.

We need, in the words of Schweitzer, a reverence for life: for ourselves, the natural world, our neighbors, and our nation.

Notes

1. Albert Schweitzer, *The Words of Albert Schweitzer*, ed. Norman Cousins (New York: New Market Press, 1996).

2. Paul Woodruff, interview by Bill Moyers, "Transcript: Bill Moyers Interviews Paul Woodruff," PBS, 3 January 2003, pbs.org/now/transcript/transcript_woodruff.html.

3. Quoted in Tom Palaima, "The Relevance of Reverence (Review of Paul Woodfruff's *Reverence: Renewing a Forgotten Virtue*," American Prospect, 12 December 2001, prospect.org/article/relevance-reverence.

4. Martin Luther King Jr., Methodist Student Leadership Conference Address, 1964, Lincoln NE, archived atamericanrhetoric.com/speeches/mlkmethodistyouthconference.htm.

5. Barack Obama, in Michiko Kakutani, "Transcript: President Obama on What Books Mean to Him," *New York Times*, 16 January 2017, nytimes.com/2017/01/16/books/transcript-president-obama-on-what-books-mean-to-him.html?_r=0.

6. Ralph Heintzman, *Rediscovering Reverence* (Quebec: McGill-Queen's University Press, 2011) 108.

7. Thomas Merton, *Conjectures of a Guilty Bystander* (New York: Image Books, 1968) 158.

8. Mary Oliver, "Entering the Kingdom," in *American Primitive* (Boston: Back Bay Books, 1983).

9. Bill Moyers, *Moyers on Democracy* (New York: Doubleday, 2008) 1.

Chapter 7

Mutuality

What we hold in common exceeds what divides us.

I've had the privilege of working with African pastors for many years, collaborating on educational and peace-making initiatives. I once led a weeklong seminar on forgiveness and reconciliation for Tanzanian pastors designed to help them deal with conflict in everyday life.

These pastors shared story after story of overcoming disagreements in their communities, including religious and political conflict with violent undercurrents. One pastor's church building and home was ransacked by members of a local mosque. These individuals then went to the police and reported that the pastor had committed violence against them. In their community, when someone makes a police report, the reported person is considered guilty until proven otherwise, so the pastor was thrown in jail, along with his wife.

"How can I forgive? How can I learn to build bridges of reconciliation with my neighbors when such things happen?" one pastor pleaded to me with tears in his eyes.

We talked about love for enemies and injustice and peacemaking. But as I heard their real-life experiences, one odd element kept surfacing again and again.

Cows.

The first time I heard a pastor mention cows in relation to reconciliation, I brushed it off as a peculiar mark of his community. But then cows were spoken of again and again, by multiple leaders. I finally asked my African co-leader of the seminar, "What's the deal with the cows?"

"In villages in Africa," my friend explained, "a cow is very important to the process of reconciliation. If you wrong someone—perhaps accidentally causing harm to their crops, or even if you steal something that is not yours—it's traditional that a cow is then given to the wronged party as a peace offering. The cow is accepted and perhaps prepared as a feast for the village, in order to demonstrate that common ground has been reached."

In that moment, I knew that I was way over my head in Africa. How could I relate to these pastors, whose lives were so different from mine? How could I share a word about forgiveness and reconciliation as an outsider, and why should they listen to me?

I began to listen more and talk less. I shared my personal thoughts on occasion, or offered an insight, but mostly I remained silent as pastors told their stories of conflict. Only after a few more days of listening could I then begin to speak into their lives about principles that could help them practice forgiveness and reconciliation.

An old African proverb says, "A talkative bird will not build a nest."

As in Africa, we need more people in America who are willing to build a nest. This is the core of mutuality, the true sharing of feelings and thoughts. Speeches matter, but the soft skill of creating a shared space where all voices can be heard will be more important in our future than eloquent rhetoric. Only when we meet people in these sacred spaces can we discover common ground. We think that the answer to moving forward as a nation is to win out over the other side, to offer the most compelling vision that will counter the vision of others. But common ground and compromise have always been the strength of a pluralistic society.

How to Build a Nest

When Abraham Lincoln was running for president, a man named Edwin Stanton traveled all around the country publicly denigrating Lincoln. Sometimes he would even mock Lincoln's looks, saying, "You don't want a tall, lanky, ignorant man like this as the president of the United States." Stanton was relentless.

After winning the election, Lincoln needed to choose a cabinet, including the position of Secretary of War. As he searched for the right person, he decided to choose Edwin Stanton. When Lincoln told his advisers about his decision, they questioned his judgment. Stanton had attacked Lincoln's character and sought to defeat him at every turn. But Lincoln responded that he needed someone who was intense, thorough, relentless, eloquent, and convincing, and that Stanton was the best person for the job. Lincoln believed that he needed to put his personal differences aside for the good of the country.

Stanton was described as being "impulsive, warm-blooded, very quick in execution, perhaps not always infallible in judgment . . . . He was a nervous man, a man of imagination, a man utterly absorbed in the idea of the republic one and indivisible; and he lived for it, wore himself out in the service . . . ."[1] Stanton carried the moral convictions of an Old Testament prophet with the compulsion of a crusader: "His abilities were great and they were combative abilities. Whether because of his timidity, his ambition, or his fierce nervous ardor, he battled savagely," wrote historian Allan Nevins.[2]

Shortly after Stanton assumed the position of Secretary of War, Abraham Lincoln was shot by John Wilkes Booth. Stanton made his way to the Lincoln home, consoled Lincoln's wife, and then went to the bedroom to learn that Lincoln would not recover. It was reported that Stanton lowered himself into a chair next to the bed and said, "Now he belongs to the ages." He then, surprisingly, burst into loud, convulsive sobs.[3]

Had Lincoln returned hate for hate, Stanton's gifts as a leader would never have benefited America. Stanton's negativity and hatred would have never been redeemed. Instead, Lincoln and Stanton found common ground to serve the needs of the nation.

When eagles build their nests, sometimes at heights of 10,000 feet, it's a combined project that can take many months. Male and female build the nest together. Nests can be up to thirteen feet deep and eight feet high, weighing more than a ton.

Like humans build homes, eagles build nests out of necessity. The structure is built for the purposes of mating, safety, protection of eggs, and insulation.

To find common ground, we must start with the necessities. What are the areas that are important to all sides? Lincoln and Stanton found common ground in the protection of our nation. In present-day communities, families who are different almost always want the same things: safe neighborhoods, good schools, supportive government, access to healthcare, homes that are secure. These are human needs.

Having discovered what is necessary, different people can then add shared values to build a common nest of peace and problem-solving.

Mutual agreement and kindness are so much better than argument and slanderous name-calling. We all value honesty, accountability, respect, fairness, compassion, and integrity. We can acknowledge those qualities where we see them, even in our enemies.

Finally, we can build a nest by intentionally and frequently coming together in experiences that have nothing to do with our areas of disagreement. For several years, President Barack Obama (a Democrat) and Speaker of the House John Boehner (a Republican) clashed over policy issues. After some time, they cooled in their efforts to find common ground. They started as friends (at least in public perception), but soon their relationship dissolved into finger-pointing, confrontation, and, eventually, isolation. They stopped visiting one another and dug in regarding their disparate policy positions.

I believe the best thing they could have done was to play golf every Friday (or go to lunch, or bowling, or something) with no agenda. We need experiences apart from our disagreements to cement real relationships and help us remember our common ground.

Rumi said, "Out beyond ideas of wrongdoing and rightdoing, there is a field. I will meet you there."[4]

The Pride of Partisanship

Partisanship is another area that needs to be confronted. As one who has both studied politics and sought to be increasingly faithful to the person of Jesus, I want to share a conviction that has been developing in me over the years: I believe that people of faith should be as non-partisan as possible.

It's true that most people have a favorite "team" that they root for. And when it comes to our "teams," we almost always see their best traits and overlook their worst.

But when it comes to voting, I believe that conscience matters more than party. I don't think either party, or any candidate, fully represents what I would call the way of Jesus. Nor should they be expected to. Politics and government have never been the dependable bearer of the message of Jesus. Parties change. I don't think Jesus would have much use for political parties, at least not in their current configuration, which has somehow come to represent a huge dividing line down the middle of America.

We feel more divided because we're told we're divided. There is a strong, well-funded effort to force us to choose a side, but we need to resist such absolute loyalties. I want to love my neighbors and be in relationship with them, whether they are Democrat or Republican, Green or unaffiliated, and I believe that most Americans feel the same way.

To be sure, when a vote is cast, it goes into one bucket or the other. But we need to remember that parties are a means to an end: a more just, prosperous, safe, and compassionate society. How will we get there?

Religious freedom is an essential foundation stone in our path. There's no single word that stirs the hearts of Americans like "freedom," an echo from the first citizens in the New World. Baptist leaders such as Thomas Helwys, Roger Williams, Isaac Backus, and John Leland were willing to be imprisoned and face execution so that America could be the first country to enshrine full religious freedom as a baseline right.

They believed that every person, of any religious background or none whatsoever, should be free to believe or not believe as their conscience dictated.

Challenges to religious freedom in the future will continue to address these types of questions: Should Muslims be required to identify their religious affiliation as a kind of test for entrance into our country? Should wedding service vendors be required to serve same-sex couples if their religious belief leads them to oppose same-sex marriage, thus facing discrimination charges if they refuse? Can people be forced to remove religious attire for driver's license photos?

One party or one candidate cannot represent the fullness of what religious freedom means. It's more than the right to worship as one chooses, and how one chooses, as a personal expression of faith; it's about whole-life faithfulness in the day to day, including corporate settings. And it's more than just Christian religious liberty. If Christians desire religious liberty for ourselves, then we must be willing to defend it for others.

How can we rise above partisanship?

First, people of faith need to think beyond their own "tribe" when we consider the importance of religious freedom and political persuasion. Religious liberty should not depend on how big or powerful one's religious group is. Sadly, many so-called champions of religious freedom only speak or act when their own right is threatened. Similarly, we tend to favor our own political tribe to the detriment of the needs of others who have a legitimate, different view from our own.

Second, we should never sacrifice our conscience that is rooted in faith. We're free to resist government if our conscience demands it and if we're willing to pay the price. Freedom means that we are free to choose across party lines in obedience to a higher standard, heeding a voice from within rather than the strident voices from outside of us. A vote of conscience is one in which we are seeking to ask, which candidate's leadership will lead to a more just, prosperous, safe, and compassionate society?

It's never easy to hold strong convictions and remain true to your conscience while also seeking common ground. But if we can identify our areas of pride and seek to walk in humility as we hold fast to what we believe, finding common ground is possible.

More Alike than Different

With all the talk about how divided America is, I continue to believe that we have more in common than what drives us apart.

One fundamental need that all humans have is for deep, supportive relationships. Relationships make the difference when there's mental distress, an economic crisis, or a family loss. Relationships sweeten life and give us hope. Relationships remind us of who we are and teach us things we didn't know about ourselves.

But I believe there are particular kinds of relationships that especially make our lives better and more hopeful. These are relationships with people who are different from us.

Unfortunately, they can be the hardest to cultivate. How do you build relationships with people in different ethnic, political, and social groups?

Here are six tools to help.

Say yes. Often we have opportunities to get to know people, even invitations to participate in events or activities, but our tendency is to say no to things that are outside of our comfort zone. When we say yes, we may open ourselves up to some discomfort, but we also become open to new relationships, new experiences, and expanded understanding.

Go where you aren't in the majority. Join an interest group where you know you won't be in the dominant ethnicity or social class. Seek to build relationships that are across all kinds of lines. Your life will be richer for it.

Lean into activities that bring people together. Entertainment is one of these activities. It can bring people together in a way that a political rally never could. Dance, drama, comedy, sports—these help us to cross racial and political lines if we use them to build relationships.

Avoid the extremes of social media: the "cage fight" and the "echo chamber." It's okay to be engaged in social media, but we need to recognize that it can be a divisive instrument, a cage fight that leads to family conflict, "unfriending" friends, and some of the most corrosive talk in America. At other times, social media is an echo chamber, people just saying things that others agree with, reinforcing their beliefs and blocking out the perspectives of others.

Focus on what you have in common, not on what divides you. Who doesn't want safer neighborhoods, good schools, and enough food? Find ways to talk about common concerns, hopes, and needs. Discover what people know that you don't know and affirm them, trusting that everyone has something to teach you.

Seek to love everyone. This sounds naive, but if we really seek to love everyone around us regardless of anything that might separate us, we will have lots of relationships across ethnic, political, and social groups. Why? Because we already live in a pluralistic and diverse society. When we seek to love the people around us, especially those who are different from us, we'll cross boundaries without even thinking about it.

Years ago, a gentleman started to attend worship at our church. He lived a hard life and had few resources for luxury items and clothes, but he took special pride in one peculiar possession: a suit that he had likely purchased from a thrift store.

The suit wasn't a standard brown, burgundy, or black. It was neon yellow. When he wore the suit to worship, the intensity of light in the sanctuary doubled. He loved to sit on the front row, and, as I preached, I would look out at the whole congregation and try to make a connection with everyone, but usually all I could really see was that neon suit. I couldn't *not* look at it, and when I talked with the gentleman after worship, it was hard to keep focused on his face and not on what he was wearing. I knew it was important to him—he wore it every Sunday—and I was in no way going to diminish his joy in wearing that suit. But it was hard to see anything else.

The neon suit has become a metaphor for me. Almost all of us have something in our exterior selves that can be distracting. Sometimes we meet people and all we can see is their skin color or poor teeth or bad haircut. Sometimes there are behaviors and ways of being that may be off-putting, and, if we're not careful, our impressions of people can be clouded by whatever is most prominent in their public lives.

We need to learn to look past the neon suit and see the person first. We need to see the common woman or man in front of us, the things that bind us together, the hurts and the hopes. Love means looking past the externals to see the humanity, the *imago dei*, the dignity and worth of the image of God in each person.

Jesus said love is the greatest commandment. There's nothing more important than loving God with your whole heart, soul, mind, and strength, and then loving your neighbor as yourself (Mark 12:30).

In a time of division, we need bridge builders. We need relationships that transcend differences and make for peace. We need a deeper connection, not just living in community but the true mutuality of souls.

I believe Maya Angelou was right when she wrote "Human Family."

I note the obvious differences
in the human family.
Some of us are serious,
some thrive on comedy. . . .

The variety of our skin tones
can confuse, bemuse, delight,
brown and pink and beige and purple,
tan and blue and white. . . .

I note the obvious differences
between each sort and type,
but we are more alike, my friends,
than we are unalike.[5]

Notes

1. Charles Dana, *Lincoln and His Cabinet* (Cleveland OH: De Vinne Press, 1896) 26.

2. Allan Nevins, *The War for the Union: The Improved War, 1861–1862* (Old Saybrook CT: Konecky & Konecky, 1971) 37.

3. Michael W. Kauffman, *American Brutus: John Wilkes Booth and the Lincoln Conspiracies* (New York: Random House, 2004) 34.

4. Rumi, *The Essential Rumi*, trans. Coleman Barks with John Moyne, A. J. Arberry, and Reynold Nicholson (New York: Harper Collins, 1997) 36.

5. Maya Angelou, "Human Family," literatureandhumanrights.edublogs.org/2016/05/18/human-family-a-poem-by-maya-angelou/ (accessed 18 May 2016).

Chapter 8

Togetherness

Your solo vision can never surpass a common vision.

My college friend, Scott, endowed with a brilliant intellect and a compassionate heart, was a Rhodes scholar. He grew up very poor. As he neared high school graduation, without the benefit of resources and connections to support his application process, colleges competed to gain his enrollment. My first interaction with Scott was in a class in which he clearly was the smartest student in the room. Scott didn't let that intellect become pride, though. He was one of the most impressive, interesting, and humble people I knew in college.

I learned of his Rhodes scholarship interview from a friend who talked with someone on the committee. At the end of the interview, Scott was asked if he wanted to add anything to what had already been discussed.

He said, "Well, I want to say that I don't feel like I'm here alone."

The interview panel was puzzled and asked him to say more.

"I feel like others are here with me, and this hasn't been just me in the interview," Scott continued. "All of the people who have ever helped me . . . my parents and friends . . . all of the people who have supported me . . . they're here with me as well, and I'm grateful for everything that they have meant to me. I didn't get here by myself."

Tears welled up in the eyes of these very accomplished, highly intelligent committee members as they heard Scott pushing off credit for the success that he had experienced.

Many people make the devastating mistake of believing that they are alone, as if everything they have done, or need to do, rides on their shoulders. The great mistake is to move through life as if it all was not relational, highly connected, interpersonal, and intentionally designed to support and care for you. The great affirmation is that one's life is part of the web of caring for others.

David Whyte captured this idea in his poem "Everything Is Waiting for You."

> Your great mistake is to act the drama
> as if you were alone. . . .
> Put down the weight of your aloneness and ease into
> the conversation. The kettle is singing
> even as it pours you a drink, the cooking pots
> have left their arrogant aloofness and
> seen the good in you at last. . . .
> Everything is waiting for you.[1]

Whyte sees companionship and support in the everyday things of life. Everything around you serves as a gift to enable you to become your best self and to know that you have nothing to fear. You are not alone. These commonplace items can remain just that—ordinary, mundane—or they can be doorways into understanding and metaphors for a life lived on a higher plane. And if these were not enough, those who choose to join the conversation find themselves accompanied by friends, co-laborers, even critics and enemies who spur them on to refinement and greatness.

"We have to be braver than we think we can be," wrote Madeleine L'Engle, "because God is constantly calling us to be more than we are, to see through plastic sham to living, breathing reality, and to break down our defenses of self-protection in order to be free to receive and give love."[2]

There it is: love. We have been given the gift of relationship, the connection of companions, acquaintances, and even enemies, in the pursuit of purpose. The point is to see the gifts of other people, circumstances, and even material things as the environment in which we can make a difference.

We not only shouldn't go it alone; we *can't* go it alone.

The Secret to Winning

Bill Simmons of *The Ringer* has likely written the definitive history of the NBA with his more than 700-page book titled *The Book of Basketball.* The complete Bible can be printed on fewer pages. In one of Simmons's chapters, "The Secret," he talks about a conversation he had with former Detroit Piston Isaiah Thomas. When he asked Thomas the secret to winning at basketball, he was surprised by his answer: "The secret of basketball is that it's not about basketball."

Thomas meant that the players who have the highest stats don't always play on championship teams. You would think that the highest stats (the most points, rebounds, time controlling the ball, etc.) would always lead to wins. Teams loaded with talented players rise again and again, right? Actually, another factor is at work in successful teams that isn't easily measured.

Ultimately, the teams with athletes who enjoy playing together, forget about their own stats, and help other players succeed win the most championships.[3]

I'll admit that this is one of the hardest lessons to learn. I was taught self-dependence and self-promotion, that the most successful people are the ones who rise to the top on their own strengths, charisma, and perseverance. I learned a subtle manipulation of people that views others simply as actors in my drama, and my job was to help them help me be the most successful. I can't adequately express how ashamed I am that for many, many years as an adult, this is the way I operated.

But I can also see now how much I missed out on the incredible benefits of finding success together, lifting other people up, and enjoying watching their success. If only I had understood this principle early on, that the secret to success is found in serving others and helping them succeed, my life would be very different today.

It's not only about finding success. Togetherness and true camaraderie actually lead to a longer, more fulfilled life.

Harvard University has conducted a fascinating inquiry called the Grant Study for nearly eighty years. Since 1938, researchers have studied the lives of the same group of men, tracking their careers and personal growth, collecting data and, every two years, analyzing information about their physical health, emotional stability, employment changes, family relationships, and friendships.

The central question in looking at these human development characteristics has been, *what leads to a good, long, satisfied life?* By analyzing over a lifespan, researchers have sought to identify trends that would help others lead happier and healthier lives. The biggest find hasn't been earth shattering, but it is definitely profound. After spending millions of dollars on research and thousands of hours in analysis, researchers discovered that it was not money or status that led to the good life.

While those things can be good, people who were happiest and health-iest reported strong interpersonal relationships. Those who had become isolated over time, with broken family relationships and neglected friend-ships, saw definite declines in mental and physical health.

Warm, close connections are essential—and these relationships don't have to come from a mother or father. They can be found in siblings, uncles, friends, mentors. Strong sibling relationships seem especially powerful: 93 percent of the men who were thriving at age 65 had been close to a brother or sister when younger. Think about that for a moment in relation to your own brothers and sisters. What are you holding on to, what past wrongs or bitterness, that could potentially cut your life short unless you learn to forgive and rebuild?

In an interview with the director of the Grant Study, George Vaillant, the question was posed, "What have you learned from the Grant Study men?"

Vaillant responded, "That the only thing that really matters in life are your relationships to other people."[4]

The secret really is no secret at all. It's an open secret if anything. Deep, authentic relationships are open to everyone if we could only remember to pursue them with intensity. In basketball, in life, in politics, and in congre-gations, working well together makes life sweeter and easier. It leads to long life and more laughter.

What would happen if our leaders on the state and national level could learn this secret? How would our country be different if people occupying seats on city councils, in state legislatures, and within Congress could see themselves as one team, with the goal of helping others become more successful than themselves?

What if people stopped looking at their own stats and focused on the stats of other people?

The short answer is that there's nothing we couldn't do. There's no challenge so great, no injustice so insidious, no power so dominant that it could stand against the power of deep, authentic togetherness, people concerned with the success of others more than their own.

But how do we do that? How do we build togetherness?

Cultivating Strong Interpersonal Relationships

I'd like to suggest three specific actions you can do this week, next year, and throughout the pathway of your career that can help you develop strong interpersonal relationships: speak words that matter, sacrifice your time for relationships, and forgive and extend grace constantly.

First, communication matters. The words that we speak form the glue that binds us together. Whether we speak words of life or words of cursing, our words define our relationships.

Aesop wrote a fable about a donkey that discovered a lion's skin. He tried it on, strutted around, and scared many animals. Soon a fox came along and the donkey tried to frighten him, too. But when the fox heard the donkey's voice, the fox said, "If you want to terrify me, you'll have to disguise your bray." Aesop's moral? Clothes may disguise a fool, but his words always give him away.

I had hoped that after the 2016 presidential election the barrage of angry words would settle. But it seems that America is awash in destructive words.

"Death and life are in the power of the tongue," Proverbs teaches (18:21, ESV). Every word affects ourselves and the people around us. In a sense, there is no small talk. Every word matters.

To form deep relationships, we need words that build up, words of praise. We can accept a culture of criticism and harsh words, or we can commit to the opposite practice of the art of praise.

Praise changes things. This is true of the praise we give to God and the praise we give to one another. When we praise God, we affirm God's mystery, sovereignty, and creative capacity for both stability and change. When we praise the ones we love, we draw out the best in them, affirming their worth. When we even find something to praise in our enemies, we open ourselves to reconciliation and peace.

In a religious sense, praise lifts us up. Praise lifts us heavenward to see things as God sees them. Praise transforms us, sustaining us through the hardest of days. Praise can flip a situation, bring light into darkness, and heal a broken heart.

We need to learn to offer praise even in the worst of times. What if the worst situations didn't bring out our worst selves? Not long ago I found myself angry and frustrated at an airport. It was clear that the person in front of me could not solve my problem as I would have liked. But it was also clear that angry words were not going to help. So I paused, dug deep, and then expressed a compliment. The result? The person became my advocate rather than my enemy, working for a solution that was better than expected.

Our words also need to be steeped in humility. When we go off on a rant, it's all about us. We're just venting about how we alone are affected. No one is edified by a rant. Paul counsels in Ephesians, "Let no corrupting talk come out of your mouths, but only such as is good for building up, as fits the occasion, that it may give grace to those who hear" (Eph 4:29 ESV).

Aesop was right. Our speech and the type of wisdom that governs our tongues always display the state of our hearts.

But there's something else to consider. The words we speak must be *spoken*. Many adults don't know how to carry on authentic conversations with people, even those they work with closely or see with frequency around the neighborhood. We don't know how to talk to one another. The majority of adults long for deep relationships. It's also true that many adults lose touch with friends, then feel awkward in reestablishing connections. Words go unspoken. We're afraid to step into the void, feel the discomfort, and push through it to relational bonding.

To develop deeper relationships, start conversations. Don't be afraid to speak what needs to be said.

Second, relational connection depends on the sacrifice of time. Some people I know will drop everything to help me, in a moment's notice, if I have a need. There are many people in my life for whom I would also drop everything to help. Those types of relationships don't develop apart from hours invested in time together: over lunch or coffee, fishing, golfing, having dinner together, and so on.

I asked my friend Paul, also my barber, how things were going with his two sons, how he was balancing being a dad and husband. He lit up immediately, saying that his six-year-old son had just hit his first home run. I asked what it was like, and he said that he could barely describe what he felt, seeing his son running like mad around the bases with everyone cheering.

Then Paul said, "You know what's funny? On the ride home, from the back seat, my son asked, 'What did you think about my home run?'"

Paul looked in the rear-view mirror and said, "Son, I can't even describe it, it was so amazing."

To his surprise, his son said, "*Try* to describe what you felt like."

Paul paused and repeated, "I don't know. All I can say is that it was amazing to watch."

His son persisted: "But *try*, daddy. *Try* to describe what it was like."

So Paul went big. He launched into an epic retelling of the whole thing: the crack of the bat, the way the ball flew over the infielders' heads like a rocket, the look on his son's face as he darted from first to second to third and home. And he talked about how he was so proud of his son, how impressed he was, and what it felt like as a father to see his son succeed.

Upon hearing this story, I said, "Isn't it amazing that, even though the home run was awesome for your son, it was important for him to hear whether you were proud of him. That was important to him."

Paul said, "Yeah. Yeah, I guess it was. He needed to hear it."

Paul was there for the game and for the ride home. He was present. And because he showed up, he had a conversation with his son that he'll never forget, and perhaps his son never will, either. The stage was set to share the words that matter.

It's not easy being present. It's not easy showing up when we're tired or overwhelmed. Most people commit and don't show up, or refuse to commit because they don't want to feel obligated to show up. It's no wonder people feel isolated and alone. But only when we put in the hours, expressing love that is spelled *T-I-M-E*, do we experience real connection and hear deep conversations.

Finally, deep relationships develop when we give grace constantly. We all need grace. Most people regret how they have hurt others, harboring cavernous wounds, wanting to be reconciled but not knowing how to be. Grace can make the difference. It can change a heart, build a bridge, and repair a relationship.

Why do we all need grace?

First of all, troubles are bound to come. The list of troubles is endless: trouble with relationships, trouble in sickness, trouble from finances, trouble due to failure. There is emotional trouble and neighborhood trouble. Grace is necessary to maintain a connection to friends and family. Everyone needs grace for themselves and to extend grace to others. Grace allows us to encourage one another. I don't know how often my wife, Jen, has taken me by the hand, looked me in the eye, and said, "We'll make it through this. Things are going to get better." It takes grace to say that, and we need grace, because trouble is bound to come.

Second, people are different. Grace recognizes that people have different tastes and various ways of getting things done. Our children, Christopher and Emily, are as different as night and day. We all need grace, because people are different and those differences could blow up into conflict and chaos without the presence of grace.

Third, we need grace because people make mistakes. Every one of us is human, and our mistakes often create problems for others. Grace helps us overlook mistakes and remember the love we have for one another. Eugene Peterson said, "All the persons of faith I know are sinners, doubters, uneven performers. We are secure not because we are sure of ourselves but because we trust that God is sure of us."[5]

Not a Castaway

When I was a young adult, I saw the movie *Cast Away* starring Tom Hanks. His character finds himself stranded on an island for four years, where he must learn to catch his own food, cope with the elements, and deal with himself. For the time in the movie that he's on the island, there is no music playing in the background. Only his voice and the sound of the wind, waves, rain, and fire break the eerie silence that marks his life. He eventually gets off the island, but when he returns, his old life has changed. And he has changed. Now part of him craves the silence in the midst of a hurried world where words are cheap.

The movie affected me deeply, and for some time I wondered why. I could somehow relate to the character on the island, even daydreaming on a crazy fear: what if I ever got stuck on an island, or one of my children did? I was afraid for them and the utter aloneness they would experience.

I realized that I had felt alone much of my life. Surrounded by a sea of people almost all the time, I longed for real conversation and real connection but found very little. I saw how I did certain things to push people away, leading to further isolation. And I also began to learn how the feeling of aloneness was not only my experience. I was not alone in my aloneness!

Now, I sometimes feel alone, but I have also come to crave a certain amount of time by myself. It's a balance of seeking intimacy with others as well as intimacy with myself and God. The one who can't be alone with himself or herself isn't going to relate well with others, either.

As you think about changing the world, never forget that together is better. Your little vision, your little strength, and your little dream can never surpass the vision and strength and dreams that develop when people are truly together.

That's a powerful word: together.

Something happens when we are really together. When we are really together, we learn to forgive and practice grace, overlooking our respective failings. When we are together, we find strength and hope that we can't discover on our own. Our world needs more togetherness—less strife and less division. That's why the dinner table is so powerful: table fellowship is a great equalizer. We realize that we're just people, no matter our skin color or political party. We see our mutual humanity. Everybody has a story, and no one story is more important than another. In the poem called "Desiderata," Max Ehrmann says, "Speak your truth quietly and clearly; and listen to others, even to the dull and the ignorant, they too have their story."[6]

We really are better together. Those who realize and intentionally embrace this truth early in life will have a stronger, more lasting impact.

Everything and everyone are waiting for you to cultivate deeper, lasting relationships. What are you waiting for?

Notes

1. David Whyte, *Everything Is Waiting for You* (Langley WA: Many Rivers Press, 2003) 6.

2. Madeleine L'Engle, *Walking on Water* (New York: North Point Press; reprint edition, 1995) 67.

3. Lee Judge, "Bill Simmons and the Secret of Basketball," *Kansas City Star*, 19 March 2014, kansascity.com/sports/spt-columns-blogs/judging-the-royals/article342766/Bill-Simmons-and-the-secret-of-basketball.html.

4. Quoted in Colby Itkowitz, "For 79 years, this groundbreaking Harvard study has searched for the key to happiness. Should it keep going?" *Washington Post*, 17 April 2017, washingtonpost.com/news/inspired-life/wp/2017/04/17/this-harvard-study-found-the-one-thing-we-need-for-happier-healthier-lives-but-researchers-say-theres-more-to-learn/?utm_term=.8bac0b9f820f.

5. Eugene Peterson, *A Long Obedience in the Same Direction* (Downers Grove IL: Intervarsity Press, 2000) 90.

6. Max Ehrmann, "Desiderata," *The Desiderata of Happiness* (Boulder: Blue Mountain Arts, 1995).

Chapter 9

Compassion

Faith must touch flesh.

I was once traveling to Nashville to visit a family member in the hospital. As I exited the highway and waited on the off-ramp to make a turn, out of the corner of my eye I saw a man standing there on the grass.

He had a sign in his hand, asking for something.

I thought to myself, "Do I give him any money? I really don't have much to spare." So I avoided eye contact. I waited and waited for the light . . . and waited and waited. The man started walking along the line of cars. He was almost to my car when finally the light turned and I pulled forward.

It was then that I saw his handmade sign. It didn't say, "Need money" or "Will work for food." It said, "Need shoes."

As I pulled forward, my conscience, or what I would call the Sprit of God in me, began to speak to my heart. I thought about how I had an extra pair of shoes in the back. The man seemed close to my size. I tried to turn around, but traffic was moving forward. All I could do was get back on the interstate in the reverse direction, go one exit down, turn around, and come back to where the man was.

Exiting the interstate again, I reached behind my seat for the shoes. But when I looked for the man, he was gone.

I had passed by and missed the opportunity. Since that day, I still feel a tinge of shame when I think about how I looked away rather than seeing a need. I have often thought to myself that Jesus was standing on the side of the road, asking me for a pair of shoes. And I turned away.

I was in seminary at the time. All those religious courses. All those Bible classes and theology. How did I miss the greatest commandment to love God with all my heart, mind, soul, and strength? How did I miss the command to love my neighbor as myself? How did I miss the command of Jesus to show mercy?

Before the crucifixion, Jesus told a parable that is commonly called "the sheep and the goats." In this story, a great king stands before all the nations to judge those who can enter the kingdom or not, and the king separates them as a shepherd would separate sheep from goats. The king says to those on one side,

> "Come, you who are blessed by my Father, inherit the kingdom prepared for you from the foundation of the world. For I was hungry and you gave me food, I was thirsty and you gave me drink, I was a stranger and you welcomed me, I was naked and you clothed me, I was sick and you visited me, I was in prison and you came to me." Then [Jesus said] the righteous will answer him, saying, "Lord, when did we see you hungry and feed you, or thirsty and give you drink? And when did we see you a stranger and welcome you, or naked and clothe you? And when did we see you sick or in prison and visit you?" And the king will answer them, "Truly, I say to you, as you did it to one of the least of these my brothers, you did it to me."

But to those on the other side, the king has a very different response:

> "Depart from me, you cursed, into the eternal fire prepared for the devil and his angels. For I was hungry and you gave me no food, I was thirsty and you gave me no drink, I was a stranger and you did not welcome me, naked and you did not clothe me, sick and in prison and you did not visit me." Then they also will answer, saying, "Lord, when did we see you hungry or thirsty or a stranger or naked or sick or in prison, and did not minister to you?" Then he will answer them, saying, "Truly, I say to you, as you did not do it to one of the least of these, you did not do it to me." And [Jesus said] these will go away into eternal punishment, but the righteous into eternal life (Matt 25:31-46, ESV).

We wonder sometimes where God is in the world. Jesus taught that God is often disguised in the poor, the broken, the helpless, and the hopeless people of the earth. We encounter God, and turn away from God, when we turn away from the stranger, the outcast, the sick, and the prisoner.

The choice is ours. We can turn away, or we can turn toward in compassion. What if these everyday decisions really do have eternal consequences?

Kissing the Leper

As a young, wealthy Italian at the beginning of the thirteenth century, Francis of Assisi believed that he heard God saying, "Francis, all the things you once loved in the flesh you must now despise, and from those things you formerly loathed you will drink great sweetness and immeasurable delight."

Francis did more than reflect on these words; he applied them in a stunning and beautiful fashion. He rode his horse from town and encountered a person that he despised—a leper. At one time untreatable, this horrific disease involves bacteria infecting the nerves and then destroying them one by one, especially in the cooler parts of the body like toes, fingers, and earlobes.

"Nothing disgusted me like seeing the victims of leprosy," Francis wrote of his life before a dramatic conversion in the direction of compassion.

Remembering how he would come to love that which he loathed and filled with joy at his newfound faith, Francis leapt from his horse. He knelt before the leper, the story goes, and proceeded to kiss his diseased, pale hand.

He then gave the leper money, jumped back on his horse, and rode to a local leper colony. Francis "begged their pardon for having so often despised them" and refused to leave until he had joyfully embraced and kissed each of them.

His life to follow would involve service and sacrifice on behalf of others, inspiring even the leader of the Catholic church to make faith incarnate.

Some scoff at stories of conversion and transformation, but almost every human experiences it at one time or another. Conversion speaks of changing from one state to another, literally turning in a different direction. We may experience a conversion to a different political philosophy, to a different religion, or to a different lifestyle, but almost all of us experience at least one conversion moment.

And don't we desire to be changed? We may want to be more compassionate, to have a more meaningful line of work, to be more loving, to make a difference.

And yet the process of how conversion takes place can be mysterious. We may be forced to change through adverse circumstances, resistant at first but later grateful for the hardship that created a change in us that we knew needed to happen. Or we may desire a change for years and years and finally, feeling so exhausted and defeated by the old way, we know that it's time to turn in a different direction.

When you can't go forward and you can't go backward but you can't stand still, the only thing you can do is take that first step, like Francis. Then you take the next one, and the next one.

Transformation often involves a moment like kissing a leper. Faith must touch flesh. Conversion must go beyond the superficial and become explicit action.

I believe that our culture needs a compassion conversion.

We've embraced the consumeristic, individualistic, and egotistic life as the end all of the American Dream. Somehow we got confused along the way, forgetting that our relationship to one another has always held a higher value than the dollar. Being human is about connection. Everyday, regardless of how much money or power someone has, every person has the opportunity to change someone else's life through compassion.

Compassion means "to suffer with." It is to take on someone's else's burden, sharing their load. Henri Nouwen said,

> Compassion asks us to go where it hurts, to enter into the places of pain, to share in brokenness, fear, confusion, and anguish. Compassion challenges us to cry out with those in misery, to mourn with those who are lonely, to weep with those in tears. Compassion requires us to be weak with the weak, vulnerable with the vulnerable, and powerless with the powerless. Compassion means full immersion in the condition of being human.[1]

Compassion's Surprising Power

Compassion is often derided as weakness. Nothing could be further from the truth. Compassion gives strength to others without detracting from our own strength. It multiplies hope, fosters understanding, and forges peace.

When we act in compassion, we assume agency for the lives of others. And we realize that we have more power than we might think.

In 1936, George Orwell wrote an essay called "Shooting an Elephant." The essay describes the experience of an English soldier, possibly Orwell himself. Orwell had served as a British police officer in Burma, a colonial occupier hated by the indigenous population. In the story, an elephant had been chained because it was "musting," demonstrating aggressive and violent behavior. It broke the chains, trampled homes, turned over a van, and killed a cow. The Burmese population, with no weapons, were helpless to stop the tirade.

It was up to the soldier to do something about it. "I was young and ill-educated," writes the narrator, "and I had to think out my problems in the utter silence that is imposed on every Englishman in the East."

The soldier walked with his gun toward the elephant as a crowd of 2,000 Burmese gathered to see what he would do. Even though they despised him as an oppressor, they were entertained by the spectacle and hoping to enjoy some fresh meat.

Approaching the animal, the soldier regretted the task of shooting the elephant, whose "musting" had passed such that the animal was quietly grazing. "As soon as I saw the elephant I knew with perfect certainty that I ought not to shoot him. It is a serious matter to shoot a working elephant— it is comparable to destroying a huge and costly piece of machinery—and obviously one ought not to do it if it can possibly be avoided." But the young foreigner felt the pressure of the crowd and would look like a fool if he didn't kill the beast.

"I was only an absurd puppet pushed to and fro by the will of those yellow faces behind," he lamented. So he killed the elephant.

Nobody in the essay feels like they have any power. The locals don't have any power under the thumb of their oppressors. Orwell, or the man with the gun, feels trapped. The occupying army lives constantly with the tension of a large population that could rise up at any time. The elephant has no say in what will happen, of course. Everyone feels pushed along by the momentum of what is happening.[2]

That's the way many people feel in our society. They feel powerless to change the circumstances around them. They feel pushed along by the momentum of society that can seem both abundantly successful and profoundly empty all at once. And they don't believe they can make a difference, that their small acts will amount to real change.

While America has made great strides in terms of economics, education, and technology, somehow we have not managed to solve the most pressing problems of our day. Child poverty, racism, and mass incarceration seem to be intractable realities. We can get in touch with one another at a moment's notice, but somehow we feel less safe. People have little expectation that things can change or that the future will be better. Our domestic debates seem to go on and on without any forward movement. Marketers tell us endlessly that we are conquerors, masters of our lives. But somehow we feel more like those who have been conquered, like puppets whose strings are pulled by others.

Acting in compassion breaks the spiral of defeatism, inaction, and resignation.

The ultimate example of this is Jesus. He had no political authority, no military army, no bulging bank account. What he had was infinite compassion. He seemed at times not to be able to resist helping others, even when he was worn out. Wherever he went, he encountered people who were "harassed and helpless, like sheep without a shepherd." Day by day he employed one strategy: compassionate action for the down and out.

And everywhere he went, things got better for people. Those who woke up defeated found a new beginning. Those who were stuck surged into action. Compassion created hope.

Because you can choose the path of compassion, you can break the chain of despair. You have more power than you think. Suffering with others leads to less suffering in the world. You have everything you need to change the world for the better!

Penetrating the Passions of the Heart

Philip Yancey describes a time in the early 1990s when he was invited to Russia. After seven decades of communist rule, the Soviet empire was falling apart and the nation was seeking to reinvent itself. Some reveled in the new freedom, but for others, this was unfamiliar territory. Yancey was asked to meet with the leaders of *Pravda*, the official publication of the communist party. At one point *Pravda* (meaning "truth") boasted a circulation of 11 million, but by 1991 it was read by only about 700,000 citizens. As Russia fell, so did *Pravda*.

In a strange move, the editors wanted to meet with Yancey as a representative of the Christian church. The writers of a magazine that had espoused the belief for nearly a century that religion was the "opiate of the people" were looking for answers to guide them into the future. They explained to Yancey their view that communism and Christianity held many values in common: equality, sharing, equal justice, racial reconciliation. But Marxism had created one of the worst societal nightmares that the world had ever seen. Why was this the case?

"We don't know how to motivate people to show compassion," said the editor-in-chief. "We tried raising money for the children of Chernobyl, but the average Russian citizen would rather spend his money on drink. How do you reform and motivate people? How do you get them to be good?"[3]

Many decades of communism had taught this truth: you cannot legislate goodness or enforce it down the barrel of a gun. Morality cannot be created through law. Goodness can't be imposed from the top down, because such an imposition is just that: it rests on the surface, unable to penetrate into the motivations and passions of the heart. Just and fair laws are necessary to create order, but in themselves they cannot create a good person.

Nor can education alone. In addition to the notion that morality can be dictated, many also see hope in our educational system in order to make men and women into good people, thinking that the right teaching, properly understood, will be enough to change hearts.

Reinhold Niebuhr stated the problem this way:

> One school holds that men would be good only if political institutions would not corrupt them; another believes that they would be good if the prior evil of a faulty economic organization could be eliminated. Or another school thinks of this evil as no more than ignorance, and therefore waits for a more perfect educational process to redeem man from his partial and particular loyalties. But no school asks how it is that an essentially good man could have produced corrupting and tyrannical political organizations or exploiting economic organizations, or fanatical and superstitious religious organizations.[4]

What this all means is that compassion is not a given. As much as we would like for compassion to be a universal experience, the truth is that the government cannot demand compassion. Education can't teach us to be good, although it can encourage good actions. Government cannot make us good people, but it always reflects the values that we share, for better or for worse.

We need a vision beyond ourselves that calls us to compassion, because people will almost always default to serving themselves unless they have a vision beyond their own interests.

Serving the public good will require regular soul-searching regarding your motivations. It will also require that you surround yourself with like-minded people, a community that desires goodness and compassion as the foundation for serving others.

What is the state of your heart? Do you mostly serve yourself? And how much of your time is devoted to actively doing something to show compassion to others?

Because the future belongs to the doers.

Two Pictures, Two Possibilities

In 2008, a friend and I drove to Nashville and spent a day with a man named Will Campbell. Will was an activist, writer, preacher, and prophet from Mississippi who spoke about race, especially in the church in the South. When I asked him that day what is the biggest problem in society, he said that many issues are crippling America, such as the treatment of women and the way consumerism is dominating our national narrative. But he said that the number-one problem, hands down, is race. We can't get along and we can't worship together, he said; we can't get black and white and Latino in the same room to worship, so how can we expect the world to be reconciled one to another in any other sphere of life?

"I want to show you something," he said. Then he pointed to two pictures on his desk.

The first one was taken on September 4, 1957, in front of Central High School in Little Rock, Arkansas. On that day, nine African-American students sought to enroll in an all-white school. Eight of them went together, but one African-American girl, Elizabeth Eckford, hadn't come with the group and tried to enter alone.

The first picture captured an image of Elizabeth just after she'd been turned away by the National Guard at the school. She was trying to walk quickly to the bus stop to escape, but a mob formed to follow her. A white woman named Hazel Bryan was also clearly featured in the picture. At the time, Hazel was only fifteen years old but looked much older in the photo. She was screaming something at Elizabeth with raging eyes and clenched teeth.

I didn't know it at the time, but that picture became a symbol of the national struggle for freedom while some tried to preserve the bigotry and segregation of the past.

Then Will said, "Now look at this second picture," and he showed me two smiling women. "This is Hazel and Elizabeth," Will said. "Sometime in 1962 or 1963—no cameras recorded the scene, and she didn't mark anything down. Hazel, sitting in her trailer in Little Rock in which she and her family now lived, picked up the Little Rock directory and looked under 'Eckford.' Without telling her husband or anyone else, she dialed the number. Between sobs, she told Elizabeth that she was *that* girl, and how sorry she was."

Elizabeth was gracious on the phone. They eventually met and reconciled. They began to speak together on race and how things had changed between them. They found they had a lot in common and became friends.

Will then held these two photographs before me and said, "Only love can do that."

Love in action. That's compassion. When we reach out to those who hurt, those who grieve, and those in need, we strangely find our own burden lifted.

Martin Luther King, Jr., said, "Love is the only force capable of transforming an enemy into a friend."

I heard a story about some theological students at Harvard Divinity School who were taking their final examination on the topic, "a philosophy of how we should treat our fellow human beings." The exam gave the students two hours to write their philosophy with a ten-minute break in the middle. The students wrote furiously for fifty-five minutes. Then the bell rang, and the students took a break and went out into the hallway. There in the hallway was another student, not part of their class, sitting slumped on the floor, with messy clothes and a ragged face. The theological students were busy in conversation with each other, getting a drink of water, taking a bathroom break, and into the classroom they returned for the second hour of writing their philosophy of how we should treat our fellow human beings.

Weeks later, the students received their test results: they had all failed. All the students thought that the test was what they wrote for two hours in the classroom. The professor, meanwhile, was standing out in the hallway during the ten-minute break and grading them on who approached the man slumped down on the floor and spoke a kind word.

No one did.

The true state of our hearts isn't revealed until we put love into action.

And in the final summation, that will matter more than any office we hold, any position we rise to, any degree represented with a paper on our wall.

What if you, the millennial generation, were the generation that put love into action, seeking to ensure that everyone had enough to eat, that people who could work had a decent wage, that every elderly person could live in health and not worry about safety or who would take care of them? What if you were the generation to make sure there were shoes on every set of feet?

What if you become known as the *compassion* generation?

Notes

1. Henri Nouwen, *Compassion* (New York: Doubleday, 1982) 4.

2. With thanks to David Brooks for pointing me toward this story in his essay, "The Anxiety of Impotence," *New York Times*, 22 January 2016. Orwell's essay was first published in the literary magazine *New Writing* in autumn 1936.

3. Philip Yancey, *The Jesus I Never Knew* (Grand Rapids MI: Zondervan, 1998) 75.

4. Reinhold Niebuhr, *Major Works on Religion and Politics* (New York: Library of America, 2015) 366.

Chapter 10

Blessing

Blessing others can change a life, a culture, a country.

No one talks about the power of blessing in politics. It's rarely discussed in schools, community groups, and neighborhoods. There's power in blessing, however. Blessing others can change the atmosphere in a room, the culture in an office, or the mood of a coworker. Blessing someone can change the direction of that person's life. What would happen if there were more blessing in politics and less cursing? What would happen if teachers approached their work with not just an attitude of hard work and attentiveness but also one that sought to bless the lives of students?

In the Bible, two words essentially capture the ways we approach others. These words summarize the posture of our souls toward other people. The first is *bless*. The other is *curse*. We have the capacity to do good toward others or to harm others. Blessing someone is more than just a capacity to think well toward someone. To bless is to think, feel, and will to do something good for someone else. The truth is that we are wired to bless others. When we see someone do something good toward someone else, we often internally feel a sense of pleasure as if we had performed the action ourselves. What if we intentionally tried to bless others each day, knowing that our actions would stimulate both good feelings and even the desire in others to bless?

If blessing others is simply doing good to them, projecting good into their lives, then the heart of public service is blessing. Serving constituents, serving children and senior adults, serving the people we work with, serving even strangers and enemies—these are all opportunities to do good and bless others.

I have seen the power of blessing while serving with the City of Dallas. As a commissioner for the Ethics Advisory Commission, I have given time and energy to help our city to function in a more ethical way. For my first few years of service on the commission, I showed up for meetings and did what was required, not investing much time in developing relationships with others. But then I realized what a great opportunity I was missing: being a blessing to city staff, my fellow commissioners, and others connected to the life of our city. When I approached the work with this mindset, it was amazing to see the difference it made in the lives of others and in my own life.

I've been blessed not to keep a blessing to myself but to be a blessing for others. What does it mean to bless others?

The Heart of Blessing

People use the word "bless" in a variety of ways. In most respects, it means to confer prosperity or happiness upon another. When someone sneezes and a stranger says, "bless you," it's a desire for someone to have greater health.

The word "bless" means to consecrate something, to make it holy or sacred. The Old English root word *bletsian* suggests the action of sprinkling blood on an altar. Blessing, then, is a kind of "sprinkling" of the sacred on an ordinary life. Proverbs 11 says that a life of blessing, one that seeks the good of others and delights in helping people, is like a "flourishing tree" that "bears good fruit":

> The world of the generous gets larger and larger;
>   the world of the stingy gets smaller and smaller.
> The one who blesses others is abundantly blessed;
>   those who help others are helped.
> A life devoted to things is a dead life, a stump;
>   a God-shaped life is a flourishing tree.
> A good life is a fruit-bearing tree;
>   a violent life destroys souls. (Prov 11:24-25, 28, 30, *The Message*)

Fruit sweetens our lives. It also leads to multiplication, dropping to the ground to make more trees. A life of blessing leads to more life, more blessing. By contrast, a life that is merely devoted to oneself, to having more and more things, to seeking pleasure and comfort, is like "a dead stump." What is a dead stump good for? It's an annoyance that takes up space where something else could grow. And it doesn't reproduce.

Such is the life of those who enter public service for themselves, or any other profession, for that matter. It's a small, one-dimensional life focused on self.

But there's another meaning connected to the root word for blessing: "to strengthen the arm." Therefore, to bless others is to build them up, to fill them with encouragement that they will increase in strength and prosperity. When someone says "bless you," as in "may there be strengthening to your arm," it means the person wishes anything that helps to alleviate some of the other's burden in life. It's anything that allows someone to feel supported. It's anything that lifts their spirit or alleviates their distress.[1]

Later in this chapter I will suggest practical ways that you can "strengthen the arm" of someone by blessing them. But until then, let me ask, who do you live for? Have you considered making the choice of living your life as a blessing to others rather than for yourself? What difference can your life make to strengthen others?

Jim Denison, founder of the Denison Forum for Truth and Culture, wrote in his blog one day about Tom Brady, the quarterback for the New England Patriots. Brady was in the news again not for his superior athletic skills but for something he did to strengthen another person.

A twenty-year-old junior college baseball pitcher named Calvin Riley was well loved by his family, teammates, and community. He lived in San Francisco, but on August 6, 2016, he was tragically shot in the back and killed in a park. His memorial service was attended by more than a thousand people, many of whom shared a personal word of sympathy and comfort with the family.

Calvin had loved Tom Brady since his growing-up days in Boston. His family then moved to San Mateo, California, where he attended the high school that was Brady's alma mater. Soon after the funeral, Calvin's father and mother received a two-page, handwritten letter from Brady. He heard about Calvin's death and wanted to help.

Calvin's father said, "It's just surreal. It would have been easy to send a card or an email. It tells you what kind of human being he is."

While countless people expressed their condolences to the Riley family, it was Brady's personal note that made the news. The compassion of this world-class athlete surprised them; he took the time to bless this family and share in their grief, even though he didn't know them.

Denison finished recounting the story by asking, "Who would be surprised by your compassion today?"[2]

A blessing can be given to someone you know, and of course, it's especially important in families when a father or mother blesses a son or daughter. The blessing of a grandmother or grandfather or close family friend can be the defining factor in someone's life. But it's also important to bless strangers and even our enemies. Why? Because blessing carries power. In a world where nothing is free and everyone is out to manipulate someone else, to bless another person is surprising and sometimes life changing.

God Bless America

A song that unites our country, sung on the Fourth of July, Memorial Day, and other national holidays, is "God Bless America." Irving Berlin wrote the song that many people can sing by heart:

> God bless America, land that I love,
> Stand beside her and guide her
> Through the night with a light from above.
> From the mountains, to the prairies,
> To the oceans white with foam,
> God bless America,
> My home sweet home.

NPR's *All Things Considered* featured a story called "From Peace to Patriotism: The Shifting Identity of 'God Bless America.'" The drums of war were building when the song debuted in 1938. In the original, the lyrics ask God to "stand beside her and guide her *to the right* with a light from above . . . ." But a "right" direction could have suggested fascism, so the words were changed.

> While the storm clouds gather far across the sea
> Let us swear allegiance to a land that's free
> Let us all be grateful that far from there
> As we raise our voices in a solemn prayer
> God bless America.

Berlin wrote it as a peace song, not a war cry. He took no royalties for the song, instead donating the profits to the Boy Scouts and Girl Scouts of America.

The song was originally boycotted by the Ku Klux Klan, since Berlin was a Jewish immigrant. Conservative and liberal groups have used it since then, as it has been sung at labor rallies, ant-war protests, and as a song of support for US actions in Vietnam. After the 9/11 terrorist attack, lawmakers from both sides of the aisle sang "God Bless America" on the Capitol steps.[3]

You could say that the desire for blessing is at the heart of our collective life as Americans. Pilgrims sought the blessing of God and hoped to be blessed in a new land of freedom and prosperity. Even today, Americans want to be blessed. No matter what our political persuasion or cultural heritage, we all want to feel blessed, and we usually respond well when someone offers a free gift of affirmation or kindness. The power found in blessing others could make a huge difference in our political climate. And the great thing is that we don't have to agree with people to bless them! It's actually the opposite. A blessing is a free gift in spite of someone's merit or achievement.

But we must remember that no one country or group of people is intrinsically more deserving of "blessing" than another. There's nothing wrong with praying for God's blessing upon our country as long as we also pray for God's blessing upon those who oppose us. Jesus taught,

> Love your enemies, do good to those who hate you, bless those who curse you, pray for those who abuse you. To one who strikes you on the cheek, offer the other also, and from one who takes away your cloak do not withhold your tunic either. Give to everyone who begs from you, and from one who takes away your goods do not demand them back. And as you wish that others would do to you, do so to them. (Luke 6:27-31, ESV)

Congressman John Lewis said of the civil rights struggle, "The movement created what I like to call a nonviolent revolution. It was love at its best. It's one of the highest forms of love. That you beat me, you arrest me, you take me to jail, you almost kill me, but in spite of that, I'm going to still love you."[4]

The How of Blessing

The how of blessing is simple: service.

Jesus told his disciples, "If any of you wish to be great, then you must be the very last, and the servant of all." He stooped to wash his disciples' feet, taking the form of a servant. He said of himself, "The Son of Man did not come to be served, but to serve, and to give his life as a ransom for many" (Matt 20:28, NIV). Two thousand years after he walked the earth, Jesus is still inspiring people to serve.

As mentioned earlier, in 1899, Albert Schweitzer entered seminary with the intention of becoming a pastor. He had a successful career ahead not only as a preacher but also as a gifted musician. That's why people were shocked when he decided to become a medical missionary to French Equitorial Africa. Leaving behind the comforts of home, he founded a hospital that would eventually house 500 people. He served as a surgeon, pastored a congregation, wrote books, and welcomed visitors to his home, helping them to see his vision for helping Africans. He won the Nobel Peace Prize in 1952 and used the $33,000 prize money to create a center for people suffering from leprosy.

Here are a few observations that he offered over his years of service:

"Life becomes harder for us when we live for others, but it also becomes richer and happier."

"The only thing of importance, when we depart, will be the traces of love we have left behind."

"Example is not the main thing in influencing others. It is the only thing."

And this quote has been especially used in speeches, at graduations, and in other moments of celebration of humanity's servants: "I don't know what your destiny will be, but one thing I know: the only ones among you who will be really happy are those who will have sought and found how to serve."

Martin Luther King, Jr., said something similar: "Everybody can be great . . . because anybody can serve. You don't have to have a college degree to serve. You don't have to make your subject and verb agree to serve. You only need a heart full of grace. A soul generated by love."

Blessing, according to Michael Frost, usually comes in one of three forms.

1. Word of affirmation. This is the simplest way to bless someone. You can send someone a note, write an email, or text to them blessing. I've found that words spoken face to face can often be the most effective. When you offer a heartfelt encouragement, call attention to a job well done, or take the time to listen to someone's pain, their lives are altered for the good. When you bless others, you let them know you've noticed something worthwhile about them. Mark Twain once said, "I can live for two months on a good compliment."

2. Acts of kindness. All of us feel blessed when someone does something kind for us. Think of helping a friend move, mowing the yard for an elderly person, or babysitting for exhausted parents who need a date night. A simple, surprising act of kindness can make a tremendous impact on someone's life.

3. Gifts. Gifts can be financial, or they can be a gift of your time, your presence, or your knowledge. A true gift always carries a quality of generosity. When you give a gift, what is really represented is the thought and love that have gone into that gift. We've probably all received a gift that was thoughtless and disappointing, and we wondered about the thoughtfulness of motivation of the giver. But sometimes we are given a gift that brings tears to our eyes, one that surprises us by the care and love the gift represents.[5]

I will never forget fifteen years ago when I was going through a hard time. I was on staff at a church—my first position—and it was a toxic experience. I knew the first week I was there that something was broken. I ended up being accused of all kinds of things, but I stayed on staff for another year. People were angry—many of them angry with me. On my last Sunday there, during the worship service, my friend came unexpectedly and sat beside me and put his arm around me. He stayed through the whole service, even though many were glad for me to be leaving. He gave me the gift of his presence and offered the sacrifice of his own reputation. He chose to identify as my supporter and friend, and it had a deep and lasting impact on my life.

Words of affirmation, acts of kindness, and gifts can bless people and affect their lives in surprising ways.

The Difference a Blessing Can Make

Imagine a city of flourishing trees that sweeten life, create goodness, and spread throughout the culture. Imagine servants doing good for their friends and enemies alike. That is the difference a blessing can make. That's what our cities would look like if people were committed to serving their neighbors, to blessing others rather than cursing them.

Living a life of blessing requires discipline and practice, but that's the kind of surprising life that can make a difference in the public square. Many people are not aware that protestors trained and encouraged one another for the nonviolent response to racial tension during the civil rights movement. Organizers instructed marchers and sit-in participants by role-playing scenarios for what they should do when confronted with violence and cursing.

Representative John Lewis recounts,

> We did go through the motion, the drama, of saying that if someone kicks you, spits on you, pulls you off the lunch counter stool . . . [just] continue to make eye contact. Continue to give the impression, yes, you may beat me, but I'm human. Be friendly, try to smile, and just stay nonviolent. And during the nonviolent campaign in a city like Nashville and so many other parts of the American South, you never had one incident of someone striking back or hitting back. . . . You have to be taught the way of peace, the way of love, the way of nonviolence. And in the religious sense, in the moral sense, you can say in the bosom of every human being, there is a spark of the divine. So you don't have a right as a human to abuse that spark of the divine in your fellow human being. We, from time to time, would discuss if you see someone attacking you, beating you, spitting on you, you have to think of that person, you know, years ago that person was an innocent child, innocent little baby. And so what happened? Something go wrong? Did the environment? Did someone teach that person to hate, to abuse others? So you try to appeal to the goodness of every human being and you don't give up. You never give up on anyone.[6]

It's hard to bless others when they curse you, to do good when others do evil to you. But what if we never gave up on anyone, and instead always sought to return evil with blessing? What if we tried to see the humanity in others and find a way past our differences in order to be a blessing?

A life of blessing can change the world for the good.

Notes

1. Michael Frost, Surprise the World (Carol Stream IL: NavPress, 2015) 30.

2. Jim Denison, "Tom Brady's Surprising Letter Makes Headlines," *Christian Headlines*, 5 January 2017, christianheadlines.com/columnists/denison-forum/tom-brady-s-surprising-letter-makes-headlines.html.

3. Robert Siegel, host, "From Peace to Patriotism: The Shifting Identity of 'God Bless America,'" NPR Music Articles (transcript), 2 September 2013, npr.org/templates/transcript/transcript.php?story-Id=216877219.

4. John Lewis, from a transcript of the *On Being* podcast, 15 January 2015, onbeing.org/programs/john-lewis-the-art-discipline-of-nonviolence/.

5. Frost, *Surprise the World*, 31.

6. Lewis, transcript.

Chapter 11

Tenacity

There is no substitute for persistence in pursuit of a noble cause.

Wilma Rudolph's childhood was marked by many challenges. The twentieth of twenty-two children, Wilma was born prematurely in the backwoods of Tennessee, and her mother Blanche had no money for a hospital stay. Blanche tenderly nursed Wilma to health, but the child was frail. She suffered bouts of pneumonia, mumps, chicken pox, and even scarlet fever. At the age of four, Wilma was paralyzed by polio. Many doctors believed that she would never walk again, but Blanche and Wilma would not believe it. Though she had to wear a brace, she regained her ability to walk by the age of twelve.

But that wasn't enough for her. She started to run. She vowed not to let her illness control her life and strived to be an athlete. She wanted to be the world's greatest female runner.

At thirteen, in high school, she entered a race. She came in not just last but way, way last.

Even so, Wilma entered every race she could, and in every race she came in dead last. People around her begged her to quit. But then one day, she finished next to last. And another day, she won the race. After that, Wilma won every race she ran.

She enrolled in Tennessee State University and was introduced to a coach named Ed Temple. Temple realized the indomitable spirit of this girl—that she was a believer and that she had unbelievable natural talent.[1]

Within a few years, Wilma was an Olympic champion.

In the 1960s, Wilma Rudolph was considered the fastest woman in the world. She was the first American woman to achieve three gold medals in track and field. She flew through the 100-meter race and set world records in the 200 and 4 x 100.[2]

Known as "The Tornado," Wilma rose to fame as television developed. She not only helped women's track gain prominence among American sports but also advanced civil and women's rights.

"Believe me," Wilma said, "the reward is not so great without the struggle."

The secret of her success? Tenacity.

Essentially, she wanted to do something, and she did it. That's the essence of tenacity. It is founded in belief, forged in hard work, and indefatigably lived out. Oswald Chambers wrote,

> Tenacity is more than endurance, it is endurance combined with the absolute certainty that what we are looking for is going to transpire. Tenacity is more than hanging on, which may be but the weakness of being too afraid to fall off. Tenacity is the supreme effort of a man refusing to believe that his hero is going to be conquered.[3]

Most people are just hanging on. They have no idea who they want to become. If they do have a sense of what they want to be, they often languish in a thousand distractions, lacking determination and essential effort to achieve those dreams. But the good news is that tenacity, while in some ways innate, can also be learned. Olympic athletes know that achievement is the result of both talent and effort, practiced relentlessly in what might be called, to borrow a phrase from Eugene Peterson, "a long obedience in the same direction." And no goal is ever accomplished alone.

You will never be what you are meant to be unless you know who you want to be. You'll never become that person unless you want to be that person with all your heart. And you'll never get there unless you put in the hard work see it through.

Know What You Want to Happen

The word *tenacity*, while often associated with determination, actually means the quality of being able to hold on to something firmly. Tenacity begins with a clear vision and continues by clinging to that vision, even if it seems impossible.

What is your vision for your life? What do you want to see accomplished through you?

For myself, first and foremost, I want to be the finest follower of Jesus that I can be. That's my baseline. I believe in God as a benevolent Spirit and Jesus as worthy to be followed with my best effort. From there, I want to become the best version of myself as God lives through me, and that means being a person of love: loving myself, loving my family, and loving my community. Extending even farther outward, I have a big dream: I want to see revival happen in America. It's more of what I would call a "kingdom" revival than an "American revival," because it has to do with the recovery of core values and the way we treat one another as neighbors. While there have been many failures of living out the values of freedom, justice, and quality, I still believe it is possible.

I've struggled with tenacity over the years—with both determination as well as holding on to a life vision—because I wasn't always clear what I wanted to become. How will we know we have gotten there unless we know where we're going?

As I look across America, I see problems that can often seem overwhelming. I see families that struggle with a variety of issues, from addiction to mental illness to the impact of loved ones being incarcerated—all stemming back to poverty. I see people struggling with addiction.

In *Moyers on Democracy*, Bill Moyers writes, "Democracy has never been a straight line, but a winding path full of contradictions, courage, failure, sacrifice, unity and fractiousness." Moyers's contention is that we have taken for granted the narrow escapes and possible dissolution of our democracy, inviting a real breakdown in community life. He continues, "We don't have to look far to see the cracks in that growing divide: an economic fissure between the wealthiest and poorest, a political chasm between tea-party republicans and ultra-liberal democrats, a social breach over such issues as gun control and climate change, and a community fracture over racially-segregated neighborhoods, schools and churches."[4]

Moyers is especially critical of the power associated with people who have vast resources, money that most people can barely imagine. The result is that justice is unevenly distributed and there is a serious drifting away from Lincoln's sacred belief in government "of the people, by the people, and for the people."

I have no illusions of a perfectly balanced system, either practiced in the past or imagine for the future. My concern is that we have stopped trying, choosing short-term gains over long-term societal development. We've plunged into a death spiral of partisan divide, and I agree with Moyers: the dissolution of our democracy is not impossible unless we change our ways.

Writing about healthcare reform, columnist E. J. Dionne said, "The politics of tenacity accepts that some problems are excruciatingly difficult, and resolves to deal with them anyway."[5]

America needs tenacious men and women who have a clear vision for how America can be different.

Enthusiasm

At the checkout counter of a grocery store near my home, I watched as pleasant but subdued shoppers marched forward and placed their items on the conveyer belt. It would have been unmemorable except for the constant commentary offered by the worker scanning and bagging the items.

"Ooh, this looks really good! I was going to buy some, too, before I go home after work."

"These flowers are beautiful! She's going to love them. Got a date tonight?"

"I am so addicted to this stuff. I eat it every morning on my toast."

I could see the difference her tone and posture made. Smiles emerged on forlorn faces, and no one was bothered by the wait. She reminded me that every kind of work carries the possibility of making the lives of others better.

That's the power of enthusiasm. Enthusiasm can make dull work glow, an office come to life, a cause pulse with the possibility of success.

I'm concerned that cynicism is on the rise. People often express cynicism about politics, about the environment, about societal challenges such as racial division, and about their own lives. The word "cool" could mark these personalities—neither hot nor cold, neither expectant for a better day nor willing to give in to despair. These people have dreams, but they don't pursue them with passion for fear of failure or disappointment.

But Ralph Waldo Emerson wrote, "Nothing great was ever achieved without enthusiasm."[6]

The word "enthusiasm" springs from a divine origin. The Greek *enthus* means "possessed by a god, inspired," with the root word *theos*, or "god," at its heart. Enthusiasm could be translated *the God inside*. At one time, an enthusiastic person was believed to house the indwelling Spirit of God.

The word "atheist" shares the same root but carries the opposite meaning. Of course, many atheists live with much passion and vitality, accomplishing great things on behalf of others. The word "enthusiasm" no longer speaks only to a Spirit-filled reality; it also indicates zest for life and energy toward a cause.

We all crave that dynamic, full, abundant life. We would all say that enthusiasm is better than apathy, indifference, and the ordinary, dull march of mediocrity.

So how's your level of enthusiasm?

Norman Vincent Peale, who wrote extensively on the power of positive thinking, said, "Enthusiasm can be aroused by two things: first, an ideal that captures your imagination by storm, and second, a definite, workable plan to put that ideal into practice."[7]

Essentially, enthusiasm needs a source. It's something that is stirred and sustained inside of you, but not something that is self-generated. As an artist needs a muse, enthusiasm needs an ideal. An ideal without a plan will only lead to disappointment and disillusionment. But an ideal with a plan, infused with enthusiasm, can change the world.

Those who live with enthusiasm seem to understand that the secret of a full life is found in embracing each day with vigor, believing that they can overcome challenges and enjoying every minute of it.

There Is No Magic Bullet

Peale suggests that enthusiasm can be stoked notionally with an idea, but also through persistent action that nudges a dream into reality. We need dreamers, but we also need doers. Just about everyone has a great idea from time to time. But the one who gets busy making that idea a reality is the one who makes a difference and shapes the future.

Sometimes we can be lulled into thinking there is a magic bullet, some extraordinary inspiration, plan, or organization that can fix every problem, or at least one particular problem. But that's an illusion.

The term "magic bullet" was popularized by Paul Ehrlich, a German scientist who won the Nobel Prize in Physiology or Medicine in 1908. He worked especially in the area of chemotherapy, coining that term to describe the treatment of cancer cells through chemicals. He dreamed of a "magic bullet" that could target and kill cancer. A "bullet" symbolizes power, and "magic" speaks to specificity and precision in killing cancer cells while leaving normal cells unharmed.

Many chemicals have been proven to extend lives through the remission of cancer and even to cause the elimination of cancer in many patients, but we have yet to find a universal cure for cancer.

We'd like to think that all problems have a scientific fix, but most problems do not. There is no magic bullet for weight loss, climate change, or relationship harmony. Certainly in the area of politics, there is no one technique, tip, or tool that can resolve complex dilemmas.

When it comes to seeing our dreams realized, there is no magic bullet, unless hard work and perseverance are magic. Even then, it's more like a regular, consistent bullet that you load and fire every day.

Be a dreamer, but also be a doer. What you say you're about and what you actually do are different things.

Calvin Coolidge is thought to have said,

> Nothing in this world can take the place of persistence. Talent will not; nothing is more common than unsuccessful people with talent. Genius will not; unrewarded genius is almost a proverb. Education will not; the world is full of educated derelicts. Tenacity and determination alone are omnipotent. The slogan "press on" has solved and always will solve the problems of the human race.[8]

When I feel stuck, wondering what to do next and doubting if a dream is going to come to pass, I just get moving. I do something that moves the dream in the direction I want it to go. And the more that I do that, the closer I get to realizing the dream. Be assured that none of your dreams will be accomplished apart from hard work.

The Man in the Arena

On April 23, 1910, Theodore Roosevelt gave a speech that would become one of the most celebrated of his career. Roosevelt had left the presidential office in 1909, traveling and hunting in Africa for a year before going on a speaking tour across Europe. In Paris, Roosevelt stopped at the Sorbonne to address a crowd of dignitaries with a message, part of which would become known as "The Man in the Arena."

Roosevelt talked about his own family history, human rights, war, and citizenship responsibilities. But then he began to discuss the impact of cynicism on individuals and on society. "The poorest way to face life is to face it with a sneer," he said. "A cynical habit of thought and speech, a readiness to criticize work which the critic himself never tries to perform, an intellectual aloofness which will not accept contact with life's realities—all these are marks, not . . . of superiority but of weakness."

Then he launched into a passage that would inspire and encourage generations to come:

> It is not the critic who counts; not the man who points out how the strong man stumbles, or where the doer of deeds could have done them better. The credit belongs to the man who is actually in the arena, whose face is marred by dust and sweat and blood; who strives valiantly; who errs, who comes short again and again, because there is no effort without error and shortcoming; but who does actually strive to do the deeds; who knows great enthusiasms, the great devotions; who spends himself in a worthy cause; who at the best knows in the end the triumph of high achievement, and who at the worst, if he fails, at least fails while daring greatly, so that his place shall never be with those cold and timid souls who neither know victory nor defeat.[9]

The world is full of cold and timid souls, naysayers, and detractors. Most people give in and give up way too early, forgoing their chances to achieve great things.

So go for the great enthusiasms, the great devotions. Go for a great and noble cause, and offer your best effort.

Be tenacious.

Notes

1. Norman Vincent Peale, "A Gold Medal in Positive Thinking," *Guideposts* (online), 1 July 2008, guideposts.org/better-living/entertainment/sports/a-gold-medal-in-positive-thinking.

2. KeriLynn Engel, "Wilma Rudolph, Olympic Gold Medalist and Civil Rights Pioneer," *Amazing Women in History* (online post), 14 August 2012, amazingwomeninhistory.com/wilma-rudolph-olympic-gold-medalist-civil-right-pioneer/.

3. Oswald Chambers, *My Utmost For His Highest* (Grand Rapids MI: Discovery House Publishers, 1992) February 22 devotion.

4. Bill Moyers, *Moyers on Democracy* (New York: Doubleday, 2008) 1.

5. E. J. Dionne, "Healthcare Reform: The Politics of Tenacity," *Seattle Times* (online edition), 23 July 2009, seattletimes.com/opinion/health-care-reform-the-politics-of-tenacity/.

6. Ralph Waldo Emerson, "On Circles," *Essays: First Series* (1841), last paragraph.

7. Norman Vincent Peale, *Enthusiasm Makes the Difference* (New York: Fireside, 1967) 8.

8. Attributed to Calvin Coolidge. Unverified, though it appeared on the cover of the program of a memorial service for him in 1933.

9. "The Man in the Arena," Theodore Roosevelt, "Citizenship in a Republic," speech at the Sorbonne, Paris, France, 23 April 1910.

Chapter 12

Faith

Transformative leaders know what they believe.

I grew up in Montgomery, Alabama, but knew very little about the world-changing events that took place in my hometown until I became an adult. I took Alabama history in middle school, but somehow when I learned about Rosa Parks and the bus boycott, the Selma to Montgomery march, the firehoses in Birmingham, and the four little girls who were killed at Sixteenth Street Baptist Church, I didn't think of it as *my* history. It seemed distant, because in my family we didn't talk about such things. As a child and teenager in Alabama, there was a certain amount of shame among white families for the treatment of black people, as well as a certain level of latent racism. That was the trouble: some things just didn't enter *my* circle.

Only as an adult did I truly learn about the heroic actions of those who lived near me. And I also learned how much of that struggle was borne out of a deep faith and steady resolve to act and persevere.

Dr. Michael Thurman, the pastor of Dexter Avenue Memorial Church where Martin Luther King, Jr., pastored during the Montgomery bus boycott, invited me once to tour the church. Talk about having some big shoes to fill. Dr. Thurman led Dexter Avenue with grace and strength from 1996–2011, a fine pastor to follow in the footsteps of King.

It was an amazing experience to stand in the place where King preached and learn about the community that was organizing events in that very sanctuary.

But it was the post-tour that really affected my life.

Dr. Thurman asked if I would like to see the parsonage where King and his family once lived. We were welcomed by a kind docent who showed me around the simple, small house in a tour that culminated in the kitchen where I heard the story of an event in that room that transformed the course of the civil rights struggle.

Around midnight on January 27, 1956, the parsonage phone rang. Calls in the middle of the night were not unusual. At the height of the boycott and the transformative work of the Montgomery Improvement Association led by King, calls to the parsonage came throughout the day, bringing warnings, curses, and even death threats. That night, King almost didn't answer the phone but decided to anyway. When he did, he heard a growling, low voice say, "We're tired of your mess. And if you aren't out of this town in three days, we're going to blow up your house and blow your brains out."

Something about the man's voice made King believe that the man was telling the truth. Shaken, King attempted to go to sleep. His wife and baby girl, Yolanda, less than a year old, were asleep not far from him. King was afraid and couldn't rest.

He got up and walked to the kitchen to make coffee. He knew that this bomb threat was the real thing. Sooner or later, it would happen. He thought of his wife and his little girl, and he thought about his own life and ministry.

As the coffee brewed in the quiet kitchen, fear overtook King's heart. He sat at the kitchen table and prayed, "Lord, I am here taking a stand for what I believe is right. But now I am afraid. The people are looking to me for leadership, and if I stand before them without strength and courage, they too will falter. I am at the end of my powers. I have nothing left. I've come to the point where I can't face it alone."

The truth is that he wanted to leave. He felt completely alone. Almost all great leaders face overwhelming fear at more than one point, and this was one of King's moments. He asked God to take him back to Atlanta. His parents weren't in Montgomery to help him. His professors were far away; they couldn't help him. It was only him and God.

In that moment, sitting at his kitchen table, King experienced the most significant event of his religious life. Terrified and uncertain, he heard an "inner voice" speak to him: "Martin Luther, stand up for truth. Stand up for justice. Stand up for righteousness. God will be at your side forever."

King said that after hearing that inner voice, he immediately felt the lifting of his fears. "I experienced the presence of the Divine as I had never experienced Him before," King said. "Almost at once my fears began to go." Reflecting on that night of deepening faith, King said, "My uncertainty disappeared. I was ready to face anything." He believed that he had heard the voice of God, and he responded. He decided to stay the course and lead with integrity and faith, no matter what would come. He didn't flee and didn't even send his family to a safer place.

On January 30, 1956, three days after the midnight call, King's house was bombed. His wife and children were there, but not injured, as the bomb blew out the windows and destroyed the front porch. King learned of the bomb while speaking at a meeting that had been organized to support the bus boycott.

He quickly returned home to find a crowd of black men, some brandishing guns and knives, and a multitude of white policemen around his home. After checking on his family, he went outside, raised his hand for silence, and addressed the angry crowd. Speaking in a calm and peaceful voice, he said.

> Don't get panicky . . . . Don't get your weapons. He who lives by the sword will perish by the sword. Remember that is what God said. We are not advocating violence. We want to love our enemies. I want you to love our enemies. Be good to them. Love them and let them know you love them. I did not start this boycott. I was asked by you to serve as your spokesman. I want it to be known the length and breadth of this land that if I am stopped this movement will not stop. If I am stopped our work will not stop. For what we are doing is right. What we are doing is just. And God is with us.[1]

At that kitchen table, he discovered a faith and resolve he did not have before, even though he had been a pastor for some years. King had discovered a deeper faith, something he could stand on.

Transformative leaders know what they believe. Many are motivated by a deep religious faith. Others believe in the tenets of democracy, the Constitution, liberty, and fair treatment. Still others hold faith in the power of institutions and traditions. Many leaders have no belief beyond their personal ambition. There's no compass, no greater vision.

Often in life we find ourselves trusting in something, or someone, that ultimately fails us. That was King's experience. For the longest time, even as a pastor, he relied on the faith of his professors and family. It was only when he experienced a dark and frightening night that he had to find something more—a faith of his own and a trust in something that went beyond his strength and abilities.

Irish singer David Gray wrote, "You're going to need more than money and science to see you through this world." I believe that's true. Knowledge can only get us so far. Financial security can be fleeting. Relationships can let us down. We need what Alcoholics Anonymous calls a "higher power" to see us through.

It's critical that leaders know what they believe. Do you know what you believe? And is it strong enough to see you through the challenges of life? Does it give you peace in troubled times?

What Is Faith?

The word *faith* means assurance, conviction, a firm persuasion. To have faith in something means you put your trust in it. The writer of Hebrews says "faith is the assurance of things hoped for, the conviction of things not seen" (Heb 11:1, ESV). So faith is closely linked to hope. When we have faith, we walk in assurance that what we ultimately hope for will be realized.

Some people think that faith is always certain, never wavering. But that has not been my experience. If faith were about certainty, it wouldn't be faith. Faith is required when life is unsure and unpredictable.

One concept that has helped me in recent years regarding faith is the idea of leaning in. There's a lot I don't understand about faith, life, God, humans, culture, and history. And I stand in front of several hundred people each week as a spokesperson for faith! There have been times when I didn't know what I believed. Hardships, suffering, and world events have made me question the existence and nature of God, in spite of years of being part of a congregation, majoring in religion in college, and going to seminary.

But rather than leaning out when my belief is shaken, I try to lean in. I keep trusting and hoping, even when the way is unclear. I keep praying. I keep seeking to understand and to find peace without walking way.

The reason I keep leaning in is because I've tried leaning out before and have only found myself more confused and alone. Some people I know have walked away from faith, especially religious faith. But I don't see more peace in these people. Instead I usually see a deep longing to believe along with a rejection of anything that vaguely resembles the faith of their youth.

In Bowen family systems theory, when one family member chooses "emotional cutoff" from another family member (or the whole family), it causes deep pain. But the strange thing is that even though the person chooses to "cut off," they still think about the relationship frequently and experience sadness and even depression due to the separation. Essentially, cutoff doesn't turn off the longing to be in relationship.

I believe this happens to many people when it comes to rejecting God and choosing to lean out in matters of faith. They still want faith; they want to believe.

The truth is that faith is messy. It's never a straight path. Instead, faith is an ongoing dialogue in which we wrestle with the nature of the world, ourselves, and God.

Abraham Lincoln appears to have experienced a similar kind of journey. His faith is an enigma, but he couldn't shake the necessity of wrestling with questions of faith. He grew up poor in the upper South and lower Midwest without any kind of privilege or formal education. His family didn't have many books, but they did have a Bible, which Lincoln read fervently. His political speeches were later peppered with biblical imagery and allusions.

Even so, Lincoln grew up in Illinois as a kind of "frontier spiritualist," more of a Universalist who believed in eventual salvation for everyone. After the death of his four-year-old, he regularly attended a Presbyterian church but never joined. He rarely mentioned Jesus in his public statements and had little use for Christian creeds or statements of faith. Lincoln used more than thirty names for God, however, in his speeches, including "Almighty Being" and "Father of Mercies."

Lincoln leaned in to faith as president, not away from it. The horrors of war made him question the providence of God and which side God was on, and he concluded that God's purposes were higher than any one side's favor. When considering the emancipation of slaves from the South, he wrote a treatise called "Meditation on the Divine Will." In it, he said this about war:

> The will of God prevails. In great contests each party claims to act in accordance with the will of God. Both *may* be, and one *must* be, wrong. God cannot be *for* and *against* the same thing at the same time. In the present civil war it is quite possible that God's purpose is something different from the purpose of either party—and yet the human instrumentalities, working just as they do, are of the best adaptation to effect His purpose. I am almost ready to say that this is probably true—that

God wills this contest, and wills that it shall not end yet. By his mere great power, on the minds of the now contestants, He could have either *saved* or *destroyed* the Union without a human contest. Yet the contest began. And, having begun He could give the final victory to either side any day. Yet the contest proceeds.[3]

Lincoln was arguing with God, thinking through his own belief. He was working through the weighty concepts of divine will, justice, and what it means to be a leader in such harrowing times. He was wrestling with questions that have no easy answers.[4]

Spiritual but Not Religious

Many would say, to use a modern phrase, that Lincoln was "spiritual but not religious." Such a posture should be celebrated as an expression of heartfelt belief and longing, but it should also be considered with a word of caution.

I recently noticed a woman's tattoo decorating all of her forearm, a colorful array of plants, birds, and symbols. I asked her what it meant to her. She said she didn't know, just that it was a way of expressing what she believed. She said it represented her spiritual side. I commented on how beautiful it looked. It obviously spoke to an important part of her identity. In other conversations, she has told me that she's not particularly religious. But clearly, there is a vital, deep spiritual side to her life.

Almost every week, I meet someone who describes himself or herself as "spiritual but not religious." By this, people mean that they believe in something beyond themselves. They acknowledge mystery and wonder. They often pray, but without understanding (or wanting to understand) what happens when they do. They value community. They think about the meaning of life. They connect with nature. The vast majority believe in a universal being or Spirit. They often recognize the importance of religious communities and the help given to the needy. But what about organized religion? Not interested.

While it's troubling to many religious people that so many spiritual people don't want a thing to do with church, I want to advocate a different position. We should celebrate when people are "spiritual but not religious."

We should celebrate because we have much to learn from those who have marched out of the church into the fresh air of the world. It's not always a choice in favor of comfort, entertainment, and wild living. Many reject wealth and the worship of gadgets in order to feed the hungry and teach in the inner city. They're not rejecting God necessarily—just easy answers that don't satisfy their soul search.

We should celebrate because the spiritual but not religious can remind us of what truly matters. They serve as a corrective to a church that has in many ways forgotten itself, choosing judgment, control, lack of creativity, and restriction rather than beauty, life, joy, and freedom.

Finally, we should celebrate because the spiritual but not religious are on a quest. While many people are truly lost, many others are searching in science, in art, in dialogue, in education. They're decorating their bodies to give expression to what's in their hearts. They're setting up altars in the world. All great quests have strange turns, pitfalls, and stunning vistas. Those who are spiritual but not religious relish the journey. Many religious people have their sights on the destination such that they don't enjoy the ride.

So, when someone takes on the posture of being "spiritual but not religious," we can celebrate their quest for beauty and wonder, their longing for faith, and their courage for not accepting easy answers.

But here is a word of caution: such a posture can be deceiving. It may lead someone to avoid the harder tenets of faith. If people choose to make up their own religions, choosing some tenets of belief while rejecting others, never committing to one direction, then ultimately that faith is more about themselves than a larger vision. Their "spiritual interests" don't rise above their other interests.

I don't know much about the road of faith through other religions, but I can tell you that the religion of Jesus is strenuous and demanding. Loving your enemies, practicing a holy life, forgiving one another—these practices are not for the faint of heart.

Anything worth the investment of our faith and hard work will be difficult, or it wouldn't be worth that much. And the payoff is much greater. When we engage in what Eugene Peterson calls "a long obedience in the same direction," we experience the enduring, deepening peace of a life committed to something greater than ourselves.

Faith Is a Verb

The final word I would add about faith is that it must be active to be meaningful.

James, the brother of Jesus, wrote,

> What good is it, my brothers, if someone says he has faith but does not have works? Can that faith save him? If a brother or sister is poorly clothed and lacking in daily food, and one of you says to them, "Go in peace, be warmed and filled," without giving them the things needed for the body, what good is that? So also faith by itself, if it does not have works, is dead. (Jas 2:14-17)

We tend to think of faith as a noun. It's thought of as a static thing, something that holds steady in a time of crisis. But in reality, faith is always dynamic. It grows. It develops. Faith expresses an active belief and trust in something. It is actively worked out and is something to be pursued.

Perhaps we should talk about *faithing* the way that we talk about walking or eating or praying. *Faithing* applies belief.

Faith is a verb.

I'm thinking about this especially because of two events that have recently altered my world and the lives of so many others near me: the death of a close friend and the Orlando massacre (June 2016). Faith is something to cling to and drives me to pray in each of these losses. But faith also calls me to action.

In the example of my friend, it was faith that led so many people to bring meals, share words of encouragement, sit for hours and tend to my friend's basic needs, and reach out in dozens of different ways to her family. When prayers were prayed on behalf of my friend, they were fervent and often tearful. There was nothing passive in those prayers. They were earnestly offered to God, asking for mercy and healing and grace.

When the details of what happened at the Pulse nightclub in Orlando emerged, in the first few hours many people were shocked and saddened into silence. But then words began to emerge: anger, loss, fear. Sides were taken. Common diatribes were dusted off. Words can be meaningful and impactful on social media, but they can also be cheap.

The words won't be remembered, but the actions will. Presence, a blanket offered, an embrace of consolation—these are the marks of faith in action that will endure.

Faith, then, involves both prayer and practical action. It involves reaching out, advocating, extending a hand, expressing gratitude, and praying in whatever way we know to pray. Prayer and action aren't opposed to one another. A life of faithing practices both in harmony.

When Martin Luther King, Jr. got up from his kitchen table, he was ready for the future. He had found a faith that would sustain him. He would later say with frequency, "Faith is taking the first step, even when you don't see the whole staircase."

Notes

1. Quoted by Joe Azbell, "Blast Rocks Residence of Bus Boycott Leader," *Montgomery Advertiser*, 31 January 1956, see kingencyclopedia.stanford.edu/encyclopedia/documentsentry/blast_rocks_residence_of_bus_boycott_leader/.

2. John Stuart Mill, BrainyQuote.com, Xplore Inc, 2017, .brainyquote.com/quotes/quotes/j/johnstuart132425.html, accessed June 13, 2017.

3. Washington, D.C., 1862, Abraham Lincoln Online, abrahamlincolnonline.org/lincoln/speeches/meditat.htm.

4. See Mark A. Noll, "The Puzzling Faith of Abraham Lincoln," *Christianity Today* (online), christianitytoday.com/history/issues/issue-33/puzzling-faith-of-abraham-lincoln.html, accessed June 13, 2017.

Chapter 13

Hope

Someone has to point us to the mountaintop.

The day before Martin Luther King, Jr.'s life was taken in Memphis, Tennessee, he preached a sermon at the Mason Temple that would later be called "I've Been to the Mountaintop." The message reflected on the state of our nation in the context of what was happening around the world. "Something is happening in our world," he said. "The masses of people are rising up. And wherever they are assembled today, whether they are in Johannesburg, South Africa; Nairobi, Kenya; Accra, Ghana; New York City; Atlanta, Georgia; Jackson, Mississippi; or Memphis, Tennessee—the cry is always the same: 'We want to be free.'"[1]

But King was also especially self-reflective that night, as if he sensed his life would soon be over. He talked about how he was almost killed in New York by a deranged woman who stabbed him at a book signing. The blade nearly pierced his aorta, and if King had sneezed before the doctors could perform surgery to repair the hole, he could have died. King goes on to say how happy he was that he didn't sneeze, because had he sneezed, he wouldn't have been able to give his "I Have a Dream" speech on the National Mall. He wouldn't have seen the courage of African Americans in Birmingham or that of the freedom riders.

The threats were continuing to mount on his life, and when he came to Memphis, he seemed to sense that his time was short. He said that evening,

I don't know what will happen now. We've got some difficult days ahead. But it really doesn't matter with me now, because I've been to the mountaintop. And I don't mind. Like anybody, I would like to live a long life. Longevity has its place. But I'm not concerned about that now. I just want to do God's will. And He's allowed me to go up to the mountain. And I've looked over. And I've seen the Promised Land. I may not get there with you. But I want you to know tonight, that we, as a people, will get to the promised land![2]

One of the great disappointments of the 2016 election cycle is that no one pointed us to the mountaintop. No one talked about hope, about what we can be together. No one offered a tangible way that things can be better, along with a pathway to get there.

Columnist David Brooks wrote in the *New York Times* on September 30, 2016,

There is no uplift in this race. There is an entire absence in both campaigns of any effort to appeal to the higher angels of our nature. There is an assumption in both campaigns that we are self-seeking creatures rather than also loving, serving, hoping, dreaming, cooperating creatures. There is a presumption in both candidates that the lowest motivations are the most real. At some point, there will have to be a new vocabulary and a restored anthropology emphasizing love, friendship, faithfulness, solidarity, and neighborliness that pushes people toward connection rather than distrust.[3]

Jim Wallis echoes such a sentiment in his book *The (Un)Common Good.* In the chapter titled Redeeming Democracy, he writes, "The cynicism around politics has reached a historic high. Democracy is the result of the steady expansion of human rights and opportunities, and yet we seem to have lost our belief in it or our ambition to take it to the next level."[4]

In such a pervasive, negative environment, you have the grand opportunity to be a person of hope. You can be more than a typical, self-saturated player on the stage. Rather than dividing and conquering, you can lead people with love and solidarity. You can create a new language that nudges people toward empathy and connection. You can be part of a movement that takes it to the next level.

And here's the great thing: hope is endless! For those who know what it is to hope, there is never a time that is truly hopeless. There is always the possibility of change, renewal, restoration, and new life.

You can be the one to point us to the mountaintop.

Hope Is Essential

We can do without a lot of things, but we can't do without hope. We can't survive long, with strength and stamina to push through hard situations, without a belief that things can get better.

In 1942, Victor Frankl was deported, along with his wife and parents, to the Theresienstadt concentration camp near Prague. During the years of the Holocaust, Frankl survived four Nazi camps, including Auschwitz in Poland from 1942–1945. When he and others arrived in Auschwitz, they were directed to one of two lines: those in the left were marched toward gas chambers, while those in the right were spared. Frankl was made to choose the left line, but he slipped into the right line unnoticed. Frankl's wife, parents, and other family members were not spared.

How was he able to survive? Frankl secretly maintained a journal of his experience in the camps and later published *The Doctor and the Soul: An Introduction to Logotherapy* and *Man's Search for Meaning*. Frankl believed that life—mind, body, and spirit—can have meaning even in the worst of circumstances. Through work that is fulfilling, spiritual connection, and deep relationships, humans can endure the most horrible experiences.

While most people spared the initial gas chamber withered away, Frankl and other prisoners kept going. Frankl believed that it came down to hope. He cherished thoughts of his wife, not knowing that she had already been killed. It was his reason for living, one that he clung to in the face of brutal conditions. He never lost hope. Frankl encouraged other prisoners, wrote down their experiences and reflections, and believed that one day he would be able to share what had happened to them. His books based on those experiences continue to inspire today.

It's hard to imagine the circumstances within a concentration camp. But it's also hard to imagine what it's like to be hungry or to be afraid in one's neighborhood. One in five children live below the poverty line in Dallas, without basic necessities and in a constant state of anxiousness.

Hope can make the difference in a child who otherwise would slowly wither in life or, even worse, find his life abruptly ended through violence. When we give our time and energy to mentor a child, give from our abundance, help purchase school uniforms, or offer tutoring or other assistance, we can do more than a simple act of kindness. We can offer some small hope that life can be better.

Religion at its heart should hold out hope. Essentially, the story of Jesus is a message of hope. Many, many people have been wounded by bad religion and the misrepresentation of Jesus, but that does not change his story. He took his place with the poor. He taught that God is present in our sufferings, and he laid down his life for his friends. He demonstrated that suffering can be redeemed and that there is life beyond this life.

Hope is essential. In the movie *The Shawshank Redemption* (1994), Andy Dufresne said, "Hope is a good thing, maybe the best of things. And no good thing ever dies." We can live without a lot of things, but we can't live without hope.

Rather than the pursuit of pleasure or selfish ambition, what if your life was marked by meaning in the service of others and in holding out hope? What if you passed on the gift of hope to someone else?

Hope Looks Forward

One of my great joys in the last few years has been reading to first grade children at a local elementary school each week. Apart from being a lot of fun, studies show that when children are read to and encouraged to read, they develop literacy skills and interest in reading, leading to increased confidence and broadened horizons.

The teachers at this school also recognize that simply talking to children aids cognitive development and social skills. So on a few occasions they have asked me and others to create a project with a child, talking with him or her along the way.

One morning a student wanted to make an apartment out of pipe cleaners. She started with a private room for her mom, a place she could have all to herself. "This is where my baby brother will sleep," the child said, pointing to a small enclosure. "He cries a lot. I wish I didn't share a room with him." A roller coaster launched from her bedroom. Why not? Her favorite place was Six Flags.

In the end, her apartment consisted of nine rooms, one exclusively for pets, along with a swimming pool, observatory, and roller coaster that moved in and out of the bedrooms. I've never seen a more fascinating dwelling place.

The more she built, the more excited she became about the possibilities. The dream was shaping in her mind. It grew until time was called and we could marvel at the final product.

We all need a dream. When we stop dreaming, something dies within us.

For some, dreams of a better life emanate from a faith perspective, a dance with the infinitely creative Divine. Though God creates, the world is not as it should be. Humans can build and bless but also destroy and curse. Dreams of a better world drive change.

For others, dreams of a more peaceful, productive, or purposeful life come from within. Something drives these people to believe that the world should be better. They're on a quest toward a better self, navigating between the life they have and the life they want.

Wherever dreams come from, we can't do without them.

For many years before my son graduated from high school, I listened to his dreams. Now, it's reciprocal. He asks me about my dreams. Before leaving for college, he gave me a book by Dallas Clayton called *It's Never Too Late*. Clayton asks,

> What will you be? What will you give?
> And what will you make of these moments you live?
> You could be bigger and you could be better,
> And you could mend hearts just by writing a letter,
> Just by telling a story or sharing a smile,
> Or sitting and talking and laughing a while.[5]

We all need dreams. We can't live without hope. It's been said that humans can live about forty days without food, three days without water, eight minutes without air, but only for one second without hope. Hope gives us courage to begin to build, piece by piece.

Hope is the capacity to see that there is light in spite of the overwhelming darkness.

Hope Looks Up

One of my favorite movies is the animated film called *Up*. I'm not ashamed to say that on occasion I cry during Disney movies, and *Up* was one of those movies.

It's the story of a seventy-eight-year-old named Carl who is a retired balloon salesman. In the opening montage, we see that when Carl was a child, he dreamed of going to South America to a place called Paradise Falls and, as it happened, there was another child, Ellie, who also wanted to go there. She had a dream of moving the abandoned neighborhood house that was their "clubhouse" to Paradise Falls.

They grew up together, fell in love, got married, and bought the abandoned house, always saying they would go to South America. Ellie had a miscarriage and they were told they couldn't have a child, so they started planning to move to Paradise Falls. They tried to save but never made it. Something always came up to stall their plans. Finally, an elderly Carl arranged for the trip, but Ellie got sick and died.

The story picks up with Carl in that same house. A lot has changed. Colossal buildings are being built all around him. Skyscrapers are going up just a few feet from his property, and he won't budge. He won't sell. He's bitter. He's a curmudgeon. He's stuck. He's living a one-dimensional kind of life, just a short line of a life. He walks out to the mailbox every day on a straight line and walks back.

On the way to his mailbox one day, he accidentally injures a construction worker, and a judge orders him to sell his house and go into a retirement home.

Rather than doing that, Carl hatches a plan. He blows up thousands of helium balloons and one day launches his house up into the air to go to South America.

There's a lot more to the story, but by the end of the movie, he's had an incredible adventure. The house indeed makes it to Paradise Falls, but Carl comes back and starts living again. There's something cathartic about launching. Something about getting up in the clouds and heading toward a destination reinvigorates his life.

What happens through the movie is that Carl literally unburdens himself, letting go of everything that holds him back.

Up is a kind of metaphor for his life ascending. What happens up there on that journey transforms his life back on earth.

Many people live in a kind of one-dimensional world. Like Carl, they are stuck in one place, or they move in a boring, predictable line. At some point these people have refused to budge or to grow. Maybe they experienced a lot of pain and now they just want to stand still and try to avoid getting hurt again. Maybe they've never known how much more there is to life, and so they move in a one-dimensional line, between the house and the mailbox, home and work and back again. But it's just one dull line.

The problem with one-dimensional people isn't so much that they are stuck but that they know there is so much more to life. They have dreams that only they can fulfill, hopes for what their lives can become.

Then there are two-dimensional people, those who can move not just from point A to point B, from north to south, but also from east to west.

They think life is great, and they've got it all figured out because they can move in these different directions. But all that they have is a horizontal outlook, never knowing how much they are missing in another dimension.

Lots of people live in this dimension. They talk about being free, but you get the sense that they're really not free. Deep down they believe that there are celestial realms to be explored and that a deep faith and active spirituality are really possible, that they were created to be not just living creatures but also alive in a world of grace and wonder. Many people live in that two-dimensional, horizontal world, including people of faith.

But when you learn to go *up*, things begin to change. When you start to set your sights up, when you start to believe and let that belief guide your choices, life really starts to change. The horizontal of everyday life starts to ascend.

Up is enlarging and releasing and purifying. Up is beyond the dust and the traffic and the email, and it is vast and beautiful and limitless.

Up has thrones and rainbows and the sound of trumpets. Up is the big picture. Up points you to the mountaintop and calls you to climb it. Up gives meaning to our horizontal, and up gives hope.

The question is, how high is your sight? If you can only see yourself, working for yourself, promoting yourself, you'll never ascend. If you can only see others, you'll do good work, probably make a difference in the lives of others, and finish life with a sense of accomplishment. People will say nice things about you.

But if your sights are set on the mountaintop, on the great themes of humanity like beauty, joy, forgiveness, right action, and grace, and if you set your direction based not on a small hope for your life but on a great hope for life in general, then your life will be like a stone thrown into a pond, with ripples of impact for generations.

The Curve of Your Life

Where are your sights set, then? What is the ground for your hope? When people use the word "hope," they generally mean one of three things.

First, hope could refer to a wish that someone wants to happen, a desire they want to see fulfilled.

Second, hope may be the good thing that happens to us, as in "my hope rests in receiving a good report from the doctor." The thing that is desired is the hope itself.

Third, hope may be the reason beneath what someone desires to see happen. Someone might say, "My hope is in God" or "my hope is in the educational system" or "my hope is in the political system."

This third understanding, I believe, is the area in which people need clarity. You may know what you want, the good thing you want to see happen, such as a fulfilling career, a steady income, or a family. But what is the reason for your hope, the ground on which one stands to be hopeful? Why should you be hopeful?

If you look at the Indo-European root of the word "hope," a different understanding emerges. The etymological root of the word "hope" is the same root from which the word "curve" (to bend) comes from. The root of the word "hope," then, suggests a change in direction, going in a different way.

Hope is more than wishful thinking. It represents confidence in something beyond yourself and your circumstances.

Look at the "bent" of your life, the direction toward which your life "curves," and you'll discover the reason for your hope.

My hope is in God. I have tried to find hope by other means, such as the educational system. I once thought that if I got enough education, and the right education, then my life would be fulfilled and I would have peace and make a difference in the world. So I got a BA from a top-tier university, a master's degree, and then another master's degree and a PhD.

But I discovered that education was not enough to give me hope. Knowledge is incomplete, always changing and growing. I believe strongly in the need for education, and encourage you to get as much education as you can and to always be learning. But education is not enough to give us hope. Many people haven't had the education I have enjoyed, but they have more hope and peace than I may ever have.

I have also been guilty of putting too much hope in the political system. I believe in the power of government and the importance of coming together with shared values and a sense of community. I believe that we can't abandon the public square, because government organization is essential to the working out of justice and fairness as well as to providing a safe environment with an ever-improving quality of life.

But I've also been disappointed again and again by the failure of leaders, the inadequacy of programs to assist the poor, and the way that greed and selfishness taint our political process. I have placed too much hope in humans who are just as broken and weak as I am.

I've also tried hope in myself. I've tried to work harder and smarter, believing that if I did this, my life could always show positive results. I've believed that my own strength was enough. But I can see now how my strength fails again and again, and how I can have selfish, even evil motives that mark my heart.

Each of these places for my hope has become evident by the "bent" of my life. Look at my actions, my words, and my choices, and you can discover where my hope is.

While I can't always claim this has been true, today I can say that my hope is in the Lord. Faith is mysterious—an uneven, crooked pathway. I have lots of questions. I'm still growing. But I'm learning to trust in God, and specifically Jesus, as the Higher Power that I need. That's the ground of my hope. That is the direction, the "bent" of my life.

What is the bent of your life?

With confidence, I can say that the prophet Isaiah was right when he proclaimed, "He gives power to the faint, and to him who has no might he increases strength. Even youths shall faint and be weary, and young men shall fall exhausted; but they who wait for the Lord shall renew their strength; they shall mount up with wings like eagles; they shall run and not be weary; they shall walk and not faint" (Isa 40:29-31, ESV).

I believe it's possible to soar. I believe we can soar together.

So I keep looking up. And I hope you will too.

Notes

1. Martin Luther King, Jr., "I've Been to the Mountaintop," delivered 3 April 1968, transcript at americanrhetoric.com/speeches/mlkivebeentothemountaintop.htm.

2. Ibid.

3. David Brooks, "The Death of Idealism," *New York Times* (online posting), 30 September 2016, nytimes.com/2016/09/30/opinion/the-death-of-idealism.html?_r=0.

4. Jim Wallis, *The (Un) Common Good* (Grand Rapids MI: Brazos Press, 2013) 181.

5. Dallas Clayton, *It's Never Too Late* (New York: G.P. Putnam's Sons, 2013).

Chapter 14

Love

Love is the strongest force in the world.

In November 2004, a group of teenagers in New York City had been watching movies at a local theater when they decided to create their own adventure. They broke into a car, stole a credit card, and bought $400 of DVDs and video games. Then they went to the butcher section of a grocery store and selected a 20-pound turkey. Speeding down the road in the stolen Nissan, they saw a Hyundai coming from the other direction. Victoria Ruvolo, forty-four years old, was heading to her Long Island home.

She may have seen the other car coming, but she couldn't remember later. She had no memory of the car or the boy leaning out the window with the turkey. The 20-pound bird crashed through Victoria's windshield, bending the steering wheel inward, smashing her face, and breaking every bone.

Eight hours of surgery and three weeks later, Victoria listened to what had happened to her as she lay at Stony Brook University Hospital. Her jaw was wired, and her face now had titanium plates.

She was quiet in bed, but the public was outraged. Angry blogs followed the arrest and arraignment, with full coverage from the mainstream media. People everywhere prayed for Victoria and cried out for justice. They would love to get hold of Ryan Cushing, the eighteen-year-old who threw the turkey. He should be punished, they said, his face shattered, not Victoria's.

On Monday, August 15, 2005, Ryan stood in court. He and Victoria were face to face for the first time. Just the fact that she was able to walk into the courtroom at all was a victory. Ryan pled guilty but received a light sentence in comparison with the crime: six months in jail, five years probation, counseling, and community service. People screamed when they heard the sentence. How could he receive such a light punishment, and who was to blame for this injustice?

It was Victoria. She had requested leniency on Ryan's behalf. Ryan began to weep and his attorney led him over to Victoria's table. Victoria held Ryan tight, comforted him, stroked his hair, and whispered to him, "I forgive you. I want your life to be the best it can be."

Later she told reporters, "God gave me a second chance, and I want him to have a second chance. I want him to follow a different way. Kindness and forgiveness—that's the best way to live."[1]

Love is the strongest force in the world. Greater than military might, political power, or economic leverage, love can do what no president, prime minister, or other person in power can do: change hearts. This is why the Apostle Paul described love in 1 Corinthians as "the most excellent way."

I believe that the end of all politics, indeed the purpose of all education, neighborhood associations, nonprofits, financial institutions, healthcare systems, and churches, is the creation of the beloved community.

Jim Burklo, associate dean of religious life at the University of Southern California, advocates for progressive political action for structural change as an exercise of faith. He rightly identifies a cycle of cynicism in political life that then leads to inaction, which only creates more cynicism; this strategy especially benefits those distrustful of government. His alternative to the politics of cynicism, however, is bold. In his blogpost "The Politics of Love," he asks,

> What is needed? The politics of love. Politics that affirms democracy as the way we care for our fellow citizens in the thousand ways that they cannot possibly or practically take care of themselves alone. A political movement that is grounded in the spiritual and moral value of compassion, especially for the most vulnerable members of our society.[2]

Love for that which is transcendent, love for one's neighbor and love for oneself create a deep sense of respect for all three entities and can form a much better foundation for American political life than pride (believing oneself to be the center of the universe), distrust of neighbor and self-loathing could ever offer.

Toni Morrison wrote a tragic and wonderful novel called *Beloved*. It's the story of a woman named Sethe caught in slavery in the 1800s. At one point, Sethe runs away from her slave masters while she is pregnant. She gives birth on the run, and, when she is almost recaptured, she makes the awful choice of killing her child so that the child won't be enslaved. It's a hard read, but the story deals with a hard and very real time in American life.

In her devastation, Sethe seeks out the man who carves tombstones. She has little money, but the carver says, "I've got a little sliver of granite left over. It is just the size for a baby's tombstone. If you can give me seven letters in the next few minutes, I have a little time and I'll carve the tombstone and give it to you for free." Sethe can't read and has no idea how many letters will fit. At the baby's funeral, the preacher had said over and over the words, "Dearly Beloved," so that's what Sethe wants on the tombstone. But the man says it's too many letters. So Sethe says, "Would the word 'beloved' be too long?" He counts on his fingers: "B-E-L-O-V-E-D." Then he carves those seven letters that represented a great love and a devastating loss.[3]

This is the imprint we need carved on the heart of every child, every man, and woman—everyone who has ever suffered and felt afraid and alone: B-E-L-O-V-E-D.

For some, such a sense of being beloved comes from a deeply held religious faith. For others, they see glimpses of the life of the beloved as they have experienced love in their lives and as they seek to pass that on to their children. But if we could learn what it means to be the beloved, completely loved, completely forgiven, completely accepted, our world would be radically different. There wouldn't be anything too hard for us as a society. We could move through any challenge together: life, death, threats, darkness, danger, things present, and things to come (see Romans 8).

Love Yourself . . .

If you want a world full of love, start with yourself.

I wore my most memorable Halloween costume when the movie *Jaws* came out. I was five years old, and my parents didn't let me see the movie, but I was determined to be a shark that year. This was a time when most parents made their kids' costumes—people didn't go to the store and buy them as much—so my mom started to make this shark costume, and I don't know how she chose the material. She must have gone to the store and said, "Give me the material that will best create a 200-degree environment in that costume." To give the outfit the bulky look of a shark, she packed the felt (or maybe it was wool) with plastic from dry cleaning. It's amazing that I didn't suffocate, but I remember walking around being miserable in that costume, and eventually I took it off.

It's easy to dress up the outside, and we love the idea of being physically transformed. Lots of people are seeking to be transformed in their everyday lives from the outside in. They think the externals matter the most. Anybody can go to the store and get new clothes and a new haircut. In just a few hours, the outward appearance can be changed.

But the biggest battle, of course, is within—the inner core. Learning to love yourself can be a lifelong journey.

You may wonder, *Why am I afraid so often? How can I let go of this fear and live with confidence?* Or you think, *Why do I keep doing the same thing that I know is wrong and I don't want to do? How can I love myself when this is the way I am?*

It begins with a healthy self-assessment. What are your strengths? What areas do you wish you could change about yourself? We need to look honestly at the ways we have genuinely wronged people, even if we did not intend to. There may be something within us that creates tension or even anger in others.

Martin Luther King, Jr., said in his classic sermon "Loving Your Enemies,"

> Democracy is the greatest form of government to my mind that man has ever conceived, but the weakness is that we have never touched it. Isn't it true that we have often taken necessities from the masses to give luxuries to the classes? Isn't it true that we have often in our democracy trampled over individuals and races with the iron feet of oppression?[4]

King was preaching about how everyone can expect some people not to like them, and King himself knew what it was like to face opposition. He then suggests that our form of democracy can actually favor some people over other people for no other reason than they are different or considered inferior. Because this is true, one's self-image must originate from a place other than societal affirmation. It helps to ask, *Where do I get my self-image from? Am I drawing that image from false pictures of who I should be? Have*

I been shaped by voices from the past that tried to tear me down rather than building me up?

The question is not who you have been or what mistakes you have made; the question is who you will be in the future. We need leaders who love themselves, assured in their own hearts of a healthy self-image. Only then can they truly love others and help to create the beloved community.

. . . Then Love Your Neighbors

Every great religion carries this core teaching, in one form or another: do unto others as you would have them do unto you.

Jesus phrased this in a positive way. He taught that we should not only refrain from doing things to others that we don't want done to ourselves but that we should also proactively do for others what we want done to ourselves.

When the 9/11 terrorist attack happened, I remember the fearful, angry response of many people. I was living in Birmingham, Alabama, at the time, in a part of the city with quite a large Muslim population. Muslim children were especially afraid of how they would be treated by other students. Harassment and violence against families were common. There are still demonstrations and outcry over social media against the presence of Muslims in the United States.

More than fifteen years later, we're still dealing with the same issues. In fact, I believe we're more afraid today than we were then. Many people want to crack down on all Muslims and view the whole faith as dangerous. That's not the way of Jesus. The way of Jesus is sympathy, love, compassion, and humility. Jesus said, "You've heard that it was said, 'Love your neighbor and hate your enemy,' but I say to you, love your enemy and pray for those who persecute you" (Matt 5:43-44). Jesus knew that only love can break the chain of hate. We have to learn to see the image of God imprinted on every person, of every background and race and creed. We have to learn to see the word etched on every soul created by God: B-E-L-O-V-E-D.

Enemy Love

One of the most traumatic moments from my childhood happened when I was five years old. I was playing in the backyard of a kid named Billy who lived next door. While I was swinging on a rusty, metal swing set, Billy climbed up on the pole above me. He then decided to drop a heavy wrench on my head. I actually don't remember anything up to the moment of impact, but I will never forget that moment. In a microsecond, I went from happy to screaming in pain. Blood poured out, and I started to run. I was out of my mind, and instead of running to my own house, I ran for the closest door I could find: Billy's back door. Billy's mom came to the door and tried to stop the bleeding. She took me home, and from there we went to the ER. I still have the scar from seven stitches in my head.

From that day forward, I called him Billy the Bully. That's what he has been in my mind all these years, a bully. I don't know anything more about him. We didn't keep up after the incident. I haven't looked him up on Facebook. All I have is one memory of him, and it's bad. It defined our whole relationship, and he's going to have to work hard to overcome that (if I ever see him again).

At the age of five, I already had an enemy.

Very early in life, each of us begins a form of socialization in which we size up who is for us and who is against us. Part of life is developing deep friendships while also encountering people for whom we feel deep hostility. We have friends and we have enemies. And we tend to put people in those categories: they're either for us or against us. If it's challenging in childhood and the age of youth, then by adulthood it's vicious.

Martin Luther King, Jr., had a great many enemies. Again, in his famous sermon "Loving Your Enemies," he said,

> Some people aren't going to like the way you walk; some people aren't going to like the way you talk. Some people aren't going to like you because you can do your job better than they can do theirs. Some people aren't going to like you because other people like you, and because you're popular, and because you're well-liked, they aren't going to like you. Some people aren't going to like you because your hair is a little shorter than theirs or your hair is a little longer than theirs. Some people aren't going to like you because your skin is a little brighter than theirs; and others aren't going to like you because your skin is a little darker than theirs. So that some people aren't going to like you.[5]

We need to learn not only to stop plotting the undoing of our enemies or even to stop just tolerating our enemies; we also need to learn to love our enemies if we are to become the beloved community.

Jesus said, "You have heard that it was said, 'You shall love your neighbor and hate your enemy.' But I say to you, Love your enemies and pray for those who persecute you, so that you may be sons of your Father who is in heaven. For he makes his sun rise on the evil and on the good, and sends rain on the just and on the unjust" (Matt 5:43-48, ESV). That is the heart of the matter: justice. We want people to pay for the way they have treated us. However, we would prefer not to pay for the way we have treated others, recognizing that we wrong people often without even thinking about it. We want justice for others and mercy for ourselves.

What we really long for is a world where we are at peace. But there will be no peace without sacrifice, without breaking the chain of hate.

When I think about Billy, I know it's not fair to him: judging him by one action when he was a child. He could have grown up to be a great teacher, doctor, or mechanic, helping others every day. Surely he has some good qualities. In our schools, anti-bullying campaigns abound. It's an effort to deal with the conflict and power struggles of youth, but ultimately it pushes those who are labeled "bullies" to the margins, making them not welcome. People think that if we can just get rid of all the bullies, everyone will get along.

Loving your enemies is different. It's based on a different reality where every life matters and every life needs grace and healing.

Our enemies give us a precious opportunity to practice patience and love. Because this is true, we can have gratitude toward them.

King continues in his message to say,

> Love your enemy is this: when the opportunity presents itself for you to defeat your enemy, that is the time which you must not do it. There will come a time, in many instances, when the person who hates you most, the person who has misused you most, the person who has gossiped about you most, the person who has spread false rumors about you most . . . there will come a time when you will have an opportunity to defeat that person. It might be in terms of a recommendation for a job. It might be in terms of helping that person to make some move in life. That's the time you must do it! That is the meaning of love. In the final analysis, love is not this sentimental something that we talk about. It is not merely an emotional something. Love is creative, understanding goodwill for all men. It is the refusal to defeat any individual. When you rise to the level of love, of its great beauty and power, you seek only to defeat evil systems. Individuals who happen to be caught up in that system you love, but you seek to defeat the system.[6]

This is no emotional, sentimental love, but love in action on behalf of those who don't deserve it. It is strong love, real love.

The Politics of Love

What does love look like in the public sphere? If love is the strongest force in the world, then it must have real-world application. Love is meaningless if it's not practical. This is why Jesus taught not just "love your enemies" but also "do good for those who hate you. Bless those who curse you, pray for those who abuse you" (Luke 6:27-28, ESV).

The greatest challenge facing the next generation is not the economy, the environment, or even how to reform a broken political system. The greatest challenge is whether the next generation will find a way to come together. The battle will be fought in the daily struggle to overcome differences, learn to forgive, listen actively to the stories of others, and find a way to share life. This can only happen through the power of love.

Bob Goff is a lawyer and author of the book *Love Does.* He founded Restore International, a nonprofit human rights organization operating in places like Uganda and Somalia. Bob lives out his faith tirelessly on behalf of others, and his willingness to serve in creative and even dangerous ways has led him on countless adventures.

Bob learned of a brutal practice of local Ugandan healers, or witch doctors, who abducted, mutilated, and killed young children for ritual religious sacrifices. I remember hearing of the same sickening practice in Tanzania. Like me, Bob was horrified; but unlike me, he decided to do something about it. He convinced the US Department of State to recognize him as a diplomat, so Bob is now known as an Honorary Consul for the Republic of Uganda. It's a title that was likely made up out of thin air, but it gets him access all over Uganda. He is the first person in Ugandan history to bring a witch doctor to trial for attempted murder, and he won.

But Goff did not stop there. He began to host meetings with a multitude of witch doctors throughout Uganda not only to stop their atrocious acts but also to find out what they needed. What was lacking in their lives such that they felt the need to do this unconscionable work? Their response was unanimous. "We need education," they pleaded. So Bob started a school, Restore International's Restore Leadership Academy, to teach witch doctors to read, believing that if they could make a living another way, they would stop killing children.

As a way to express his servanthood to the Ugandan witch doctors, he asks to wash their feet after every meeting filled with tension and potential danger. This follows the example of Jesus, who washed his disciples' feet, even those of his betrayer, Judas, on the night before Jesus was killed. Foot washing in ancient times was considered a job for servants alone; no one else would lower themselves to touch one of the dirtiest parts of a human. Can you imagine the scene of Bob stooping to wash the feet of a witch doctor? Bob said this about his choice to wash the feet of his enemies: "We need to quit trying to be right and start being humble. If we're captivated by this other stuff, we miss our purpose, which is to love God, love others, and do something about it!"[7]

There's strength and power in love. We need that kind of strength in our politics, schools, communities, and neighborhoods. We need love in action.

Among millennials, who will lead in the future, the ones who learn to love will make the greatest and most lasting impact.

Notes

1. Quoted in David Jeremiah, *Captured by Grace* (Nashville: Thomas Nelson, 2006) 10.

2. Jim Burklo, "The Politics of Love," Huffpost (blog), 19 November 2014, huffingtonpost.com/jim-burklo/the-politics-of-love_b_6182034.html.

3. Toni Morrison, *Beloved* (1987; repr., New York: Penguin Books, 2000) 8.

4. Martin Luther King, Jr., "Loving Your Enemies," sermon delivered at Dexter Avenue Memorial Church, Montgomery AL, 17 November 1957, available at kingencyclopedia.stanford.edu/encyclopedia/documentsentry/doc_loving_your_enemies/.

5. Ibid.

6. Ibid.

7. Wendy Cloherty, "Kissing the Witch Doctor: What Love Does (with Bob Goff)," *Viewpoint*, March 20, 2015.

Chapter 15

Imagination

Imagination can carry us to a world yet to be discovered.

On November 9, 1989, the Berlin Wall fell in Germany. If you're too young to remember the Cold War, you're probably at least familiar with the conflict that divided the world for more than forty years between the United States and the Soviet Union. It was "cold" because there was little fighting, although nuclear arms were developed to an extent that the world could have been destroyed many times over. After World War II and up to 1961, Berlin, Germany, was occupied by both Russian and American forces, but then Russian forces demanded that the Americans leave, and the compromise was that they built a massive wall to split East and West Germany.

I traveled to Berlin a year and a half before the wall came down. I remember seeing the military presence, machine guns, barbed wire. Families and friends were separated by the wall and could not visit one another. On the eastern, Soviet side, no one could escape; no one could travel. It was bleak and depressing. I saw computers in offices that were decades old, remnants of Soviet power, with no technological improvements for many years. On the western, American/Allies side, conditions were better. People seemed happier, and the ripples of a society that continued to develop and prosper were evident. Still, the city was divided down the middle, its heart cut through.

There was no more powerful symbol of the Cold War than the Berlin Wall. But after twenty-eight years of division, the Berlin Wall came down. I remember seeing on the news people dancing on the wall, singing, laughing. Whatever fears, emotions, and reasons prompted the building of the wall could not compare to the joy, celebration, and hopefulness that followed the felling of the wall.

In 2014, an article appeared in the *New York Times* to mark the twenty-fifth anniversary of the coming down of the wall.[1] The article said that the biggest reason the wall came down was not Ronald Reagan's speech in front of the wall in 1987 telling Soviet leaders, "tear down this wall." The biggest factor was not changes within the Soviet Union to have more openness and economic development.

No, the biggest factor was the involvement of "everyday Germans" who were unified and willing to sacrifice their lives for their freedom and for one another. They held close together and kept demanding their freedom. They practiced creative resistance, refusing to accept the reality of a divided city. One of the leaders was twenty-year-old Katrin Hattenhauer, a theater major and church intern. She said of the resistance that shared suffering held the group together more than shared success.

"Where the hammer has come down," she said, "whatever is underneath is going to hold together."

Leaders of the future from the millennial generation will need qualities such as chutzpah, persistence, humility, and compassion. But they will also need imagination. They will need to think outside the box, go the extra mile, reach beyond the limits of their creativity and energy, and imagine a better world than the one they inherit.

One of Albert Einstein's most significant qualities was his ability to take conceptual problems and imagine them in real-life scenarios. He regularly engaged in "thought experiments" that helped him develop such breakthroughs as the general theory of relativity. "Imagination is more important than knowledge," Einstein said. "Knowledge is limited. Imagination encircles the world."[2]

Imagination matters more than political or educational insight. Imagination can open up worlds that were previously unattainable, create compromises among intractable interests, and tear down walls of separation.

Edmund Burke said, "There is a boundary to men's passions when they act from feelings; but none when they are under the influence of imagination."[3]

The brilliant scientist Carl Sagan said, "Imagination will often carry us to worlds that never were. But without it we go nowhere."[4]

Stephen Covey, author of *The Seven Habits of Highly Effective People*, said, "Live out of your imagination, not your history."[5]

Isn't that what we need more of? Defeatism says, "Things will never change." That's an attitude based in the past. History says that different peoples will never get along, that because there aren't enough resources, there will always be fighting, and that the worst angels of our nature will always win out.

We need a generation to say, "That's history. We can imagine a better future, and we're willing to work hard, band together, and stay strong when the hammer comes down."

Moral Imagination

The word *imagination* is defined in the Merriam-Webster Intercollegiate Dictionary as "the act or power of forming a mental image of something not present to the senses or never before wholly perceived in reality." We can dream of something different, and that dreaming is crucial to realizing a different reality.

Certainly we need innovation and creativity to improve quality of life. But there is another area in which we need imagination if we are to be a people of compassion and justice, creating solutions to alleviate suffering and bridge racial gaps.

We need a higher capacity for moral imagination.

Moral imagination may be defined as "a uniquely human ability to conceive of fellow humanity as moral beings and as persons, not as objects whose value rests in utility or usefulness."[6] According to Jonathan Jones, "An intuitive ability to perceive ethical truths and abiding law in the midst of chaotic experience, the moral imagination should be an aspiration to a proper ordering of the soul and, consequently, of the commonwealth."

Edmund Burke was the first to use the term, referring to an idea that our ethics should transcend our personal experience and embrace the dignity of the human race.

C. S. Lewis wrote in *The Abolition of Man*,

> . . . the stakes are as high as they can be. That which is ultimate is in question. Full and proper appreciation of the moral imagination reveals that everything could be other than it is. And, in fact, it will be, should

we fail in our charge. Losing control of the moral imagination is the very meaning of civilizational decay; it represents the loss of a world. Thus, I would close by reminding you that moral imagination is the name for the most important thing with which we can be concerned. Rightly understood, moral imagination is the indispensable steward for the very meaning of humanity. Embodied in the concept is the perennial challenge that defines our purpose, if only we would see, and that constitutes our destiny, if only we would act.[7]

Both politics and religion are hollow apart from moral imagination. Burke also said that, lacking such imagination, "we are cast forth from this world of reason, and order, and peace, and virtue, and fruitful penitence, into the antagonist world of madness, discord, vice, confusion, and unavailing sorrow."[8]

What might moral imagination lead us to undertake?

We could say that Isaiah 61 offers a glimpse of life as it could be, and a guide for the goals of our collective life. In *The Message* translation, this is the vision:

> The Spirit of God, the Master, is on me
>   because God anointed me.
> He sent me to preach good news to the poor,
>   heal the heartbroken,
> Announce freedom to all captives,
>   pardon all prisoners.
> God sent me to announce the year of his grace—
>   a celebration of God's destruction of our enemies—
>   and to comfort all who mourn,
> To care for the needs of all who mourn in Zion,
>   give them bouquets of roses instead of ashes,
> Messages of joy instead of news of doom,
>   a praising heart instead of a languid spirit.
> Rename them "Oaks of Righteousness"
>   planted by God to display his glory.
> They'll rebuild the old ruins,
>   raise a new city out of the wreckage.
> They'll start over on the ruined cities,
>   take the rubble left behind and make it new. (Isa 61:1-5)

Where are the leaders who will point us to that kind of vision? Everyone having enough, rebuilding old ruins, the healing of the brokenhearted—these are dreams that offer a life's purpose.

Isaiah 65, again in *The Message* translation, continues with the vision:

No more sounds of weeping in the city,
    no cries of anguish;
No more babies dying in the cradle,
    or old people who don't enjoy a full lifetime;
One-hundredth birthdays will be considered normal—
    anything less will seem like a cheat.
They'll build houses
    and move in.
They'll plant fields
    and eat what they grow.
No more building a house
    that some outsider takes over,
No more planting fields
    that some enemy confiscates,
For my people will be as long-lived as trees,
    my chosen ones will have satisfaction in their work.
They won't work and have nothing come of it,
    they won't have children snatched out from under them.
For they themselves are plantings blessed by God,
    with their children and grandchildren likewise God-blessed. (Isa 65:17-25)

Bob Pierce, the founder of World Vision, was in Korea in 1950. He felt helpless watching children who were orphaned by the Korean War, and he watched them standing in endless food lines. One day as he saw how little food there was to distribute, one of those children dropped dead right there in the line. She starved to death. It broke Bob's heart. He could have walked away from that food line and forgotten all about it. But instead, he decided to do something about it. He made a declaration: we are going to get food to the front lines. Even if it kills me, he said, we're going to do it. So he embraced this passion and started to travel back and forth between the US and Korea, raising money and raising awareness.

In one of those trips, he met a little girl named White Jade. She had been beaten and disowned by her family because of her decision to follow Christ. All Bob had in his pocket was $5, and he gave it to her. But that's not all he did. He pledged to send her money every month. That Spirit-prompted act of compassion became the catalyst for World Vision's child sponsorship program. In 2014, there were more than 4 million sponsored children.

Matt Litton, in *Relevant*, wrote,

> Imagination is the groundwork of progress. It is the blueprint of joy. Before we climb a mountain, we must be able to imagine ourselves at the peak. Before we write a book, we imagine seeing our name printed on the cover. Before we break an addiction, lose weight or get out of debt, we imagine that change as reality. God has given us imagination so that we can envision the possibilities in between who we are today and who we were made to be, between the world in its fallen condition and a world where all inhabit life to the fullest.[9]

What kind of world do you dream of? Can you say with clarity, "Even though the world is not what it should be, I am committed to working on making the world what it can be"?

Creativity Killers

Creativity is an essential quality of being human. If you ever hear someone say that they don't have a creative bone in their body, they are seriously underestimating their skeleton.

We're born with the capacity for creativity. We can either allow creativity to come through us, reshaping ourselves and our surroundings, or deny it and go along with the problems we see every day, from child hunger to racial divides.

While creativity and imagination can be developed, they must be nurtured. My experience with creativity, especially when it applies to writing and preparing messages, is that it comes like a match strike and then builds in momentum. But this only happens after I have put in the time and created the right conditions for my imagination to flow.

Perhaps this is why we see so little imagination in our politics, educational systems, community organizing, and capacity to work toward lasting change. We're just too busy, overwhelmed by the rush of "now," and consumed by the facts on the ground. Such an overworked and undervalued life leads to cynicism and despair.

We can also surround ourselves with like-minded cynics, people who suffer from a lack of creativity (and likely a real lack of real engagement with the issues that plague people) such that they bring us down to their level.

I'd like to offer ten mental and environmental blocks to creativity that must be overcome in order to imagine and work toward a better world.

1. Stress. When our brains are always putting out fires, we neglect the central coal in our center. Feelings of being overwhelmed can lead to patterns of behavior that lean in to numbing, brainless activities. If you're not feeling imaginative, you may need to deal with your stress first to come to a quiet mindset.

2. Negative people. The world is full of negative people, those who will tell you why you can't, shouldn't, or ever will. Even a few people like this who have an active part in our lives can douse creativity. Of course, we all have family obligations that may require us to bear with certain people who can bring us down, and we still need to find ways to honor these relationships. Apart from such responsibilities, do all that you can to flee from negative people, instead surrounding yourself with those who are dreaming like you and seeking to be positive in outlook and action.

3. Needing to be right all the time. Some people are afraid to appear foolish if they propose or pursue something that seems radical. And many people get stuck with needing to feel in control and intelligent. Morally courageous and imaginative people aren't afraid to try new things or make mistakes.

4. Needing to be logical. Who says that imaginative solutions are always logical, at least in the beginning? Often ideas that seem ridiculous end up making the most sense in the end. Suspend logic for a while when you feel stuck, asking, "What if . . . ?"

5. Always following the rules. Sometimes the rules defend an unjust or untenable system. If you always follow the rules (especially the correct norms of behavior and accepted reasoning), you'll never work for a better future. But beware: breaking or bending the rules, while opening up new possibilities, still usually carries a cost.

6. Work, work, work. A schedule full of endless work and an attitude that one should "work themselves to death" can implicitly or explicitly declare that play is frivolous. When I struggle with creativity, often the best thing I can do is take a walk, get some exercise, meet a friend for coffee, or get a change of scenery.

7. Thinking that's not your area. Who says it's not your area, to do something innovative and helpful for someone in need? You may bring the needed element of imagination and creativity that can truly bring change to someone's life.

8. Detachment. Being separate from community deprives you of creative energy. Most great writers, painters, and even politicians thrive on the energy of others (at least in doses) to inform their creative process and stay encouraged. Creative activity often sparks after reading a great book, learning about an innovative process, going to a museum, or seeing a phenomenal movie. Our creative juices flow from the creativity of others.

9. Disorganization. Whatever your desk needs to be (ingeniously messy, meticulously ordered, or somewhere in between), not having the right environment can be a creativity killer.

10. The drive to "produce something." There will always be people asking, "So what are you going to *do* with that?" Not everything has to fulfill a function. Not every study has to be for the purposes of greater productivity or moneymaking. Some things take time, simmering and waiting, and sometimes discovery and attempts at innovation fall flat. But nothing is wasted in the creative process.[10]

To get out of these patterns, get moving. Take a step toward imagination and allow yourself room for creativity.

Time to Tear Down the Wall

Once there was an astounding castle owned by the Castlereagh family, one of the most princely residences in Ireland. But the ancient home fell into decay and was no longer inhabited. The usual happened. When peasants wanted to repair a road, build a chimney or even a pigsty, they would scavenge stone from the fine old castle. The stones were already craftily cut, finished, and fit. Best of all, they were available without digging and carrying for miles.

One day Lord Londonderry visited this castle. He was the surviving descendant and heir. When he saw the state of his ancestral home, he determined to end the robbery of the building for its stones. This was not only the legacy of the glory of his family but one of the greatest treasures of Ireland. So he sent for his agent and gave orders for the castle to be enclosed with a wall six feet tall. He believed this would keep out the thieves, so he went on his way.

Three or four years later, he returned. To his astonishment, the castle was gone, completely disappeared, vanished into thin air. In its place was a huge wall enclosing nothing. He sent for his agent and demanded to know why his orders had not been carried out. The agent insisted they had been, that he did exactly as he was asked.

"But where is the castle?" asked the lord.

"The castle? I built the wall with it, my lord! Why should I go for miles to get materials when the finest stones in Ireland were beside me?"

Sometimes when we build a wall, we end up destroying the very thing we wanted to protect.

That's what happens when we fail to exercise imagination. When we simply focus on what's in front of us, stone by stone, we build up a defense that keeps us stuck and ultimately destroys something essential within us.

But when the walls come down, we can experience wholeness, connection, and healing. We can help one another imagine a better world and join forces in creating that world.

In Einstein's words, imagination is everything.

So start dreaming. Imagine. Get moving. Tear down some walls. Restore the ruins. Raise up a new city out of the wreckage.

Notes

1. Mary Elise Sarotte, "How the Fall of the Berlin Wall Really Happened," *New York Times*, 6 November 2014, nytimes.com/2014/11/07/opinion/how-the-berlin-wall-really-fell.html.

2. Albert Einstein, quoted in "What Life Means to Einstein: An Interview by George Sylvester Viereck," *Saturday Evening Post*, 26 October 1929.

3. Edmund Burke, *The Works of Edmund Burke, With a Memoir: Volume II* (New York: Harper and Brothers Publishers, 1857) 47.

4. Carl Sagan, *Cosmos* (New York: Random House, 1980) 4.

5. As quoted in Eric Allenbaugh, *Wake-up Calls: You Don't Have to Sleepwalk through your Life, Love, or Career!* (Austin: Bard Press, 1992) 65.

6. See Jonathan Jones, "Defining 'Moral Imagination,'" *First Things* (blog), 1 July 2009, firstthings.com/blogs/firstthoughts/2009/07/defining-moral-imagination.

7. C. S. Lewis, *The Abolition of Man*, archive.org/stream/TheAbolitionOfMan_229/C.s.Lewis-The-AbolitionOfMan_djvu.txt.

8. Quoted by Russell Kirk in "The Moral Imagination," kirkcenter.org/index.php/detail/the-moral-imagination/.

9. Matt Litton, "A Call for the Christian Imagination," *Relevant* (online edition), 15 January 2013, archives.relevantmagazine.com/god/worldview/call-christian-imagination.

10. 3, 4 and 5 on the list are adapted from Roger von Oech, *A Whack on the Side of the Head*, p. 9, quoted in Swindoll, *The Quest for Character* (Portland OR: Multnomah Press, 1998) 200. I also gained some inspiration for this list from the article, "Ten Reasons Why We Struggle with Creativity," David Disalvo, 16 March 2013, forbes.com/sites/daviddisalvo/2013/03/16/ 10-reasons-why-we-struggle-with-creativity/#7298ba5e19f8.6

Other available titles from SMYTH& HELWYS

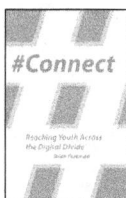

#Connect
Reaching Youth Across the Digital Divide
Brian Foreman

Reaching our youth across the digital divide is a struggle for parents, ministers, and other adults who work with Generation Z—today's teenagers. *#Connect* leads readers into the technological landscape, encourages conversations with teenagers, and reminds us all to be the presence of Christ in every facet of our lives.   *978-1-57312-693-9 120 pages/pb* **$13.00**

Atonement in the Apocalypse
An Exposé of the Defeat of Evil
Robert W. Canoy

Revelation calls believers to see themselves through the unique lens of redemptive atonement and to live and model daily that they see themselves in the present moment as redeemed people. Having thus seen themselves, believers likewise are directed to see and to relate to others in this world the very way that God has seen them from eternity.

    978-1-57312-946-6 218 pages/pb **$22.00**

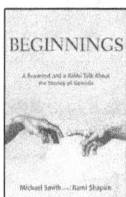

Beginnings
A Reverend and a Rabbi Talk About the Stories of Genesis
Michael Smith and Rami Shapiro

Editor Aaron Herschel Shapiro declares that stories "must be retold—not just repeated, but reinvented, reimagined, and reexperienced" to remain vital in the world. Mike and Rami continue their conversations from the *Mount and Mountain* books, exploring the places where their traditions intersect and diverge, listening to each other as they respond to the stories of Genesis.   *978-1-57312-772-1 202 pages/pb* **$18.00**

Bugles in the Afternoon
Dealing with Discouragement and Disillusionment in Ministry
Judson Edwards

In *Bugles in the Afternoon*, Edwards writes, "My long experience in the church has convinced me that most ministers—both professional and lay—spend time under the juniper tree. Those ministers who have served more than ten years and not been depressed, discouraged, or disillusioned can hold their annual convention in a phone booth."

    978-1-57312-865-0 148 pages/pb **$16.00**

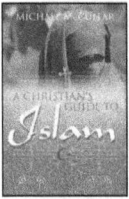

A Christian's Guide to Islam
Michael D. McCullar

A Christian's Guide to Islam provides a brief but accurate guide to Muslim formation, history, structure, beliefs, practices, and goals. It explores to what degree the tenets of Islam have been misinterpreted, corrupted, or abused over the centuries.

978-1-57312-512-3 128 pages/pb **$16.00**

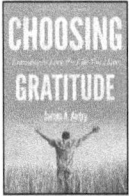

Choosing Gratitude
Learning to Love the Life You Have

James A. Autry

Autry reminds us that gratitude is a choice, a spiritual—not social—process. He suggests that if we cultivate gratitude as a way of being, we may not change the world and its ills, but we can change our response to the world. If we fill our lives with moments of gratitude, we will indeed love the life we have.

978-1-57312-614-4 144 pages/pb **$15.00**

Choosing Gratitude 365 Days a Year
Your Daily Guide to Grateful Living

James A. Autry and Sally J. Pederson

Filled with quotes, poems, and the inspired voices of both Pederson and Autry, in a society consumed by fears of not having "enough"—money, possessions, security, and so on—this book suggests that if we cultivate gratitude as a way of being, we may not change the world and its ills, but we can change our response to the world.

978-1-57312-689-2 210 pages/pb **$18.00**

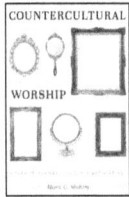

Countercultural Worship
A Plea to Evangelicals in a Secular Age

Mark G. McKim

Evangelical worship, McKim argues, has drifted far from both its biblical roots and historic origins, leaving evangelicals in danger of becoming mere chaplains to the wider culture, oblivious to the contradictions between what the secular culture says is real and important and what Scripture says is real and important.

978-1-57312-873-5 174 pages/pb **$19.00**

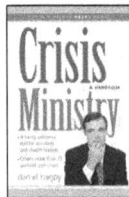

Crisis Ministry: A Handbook
Daniel G. Bagby

Covering more than 25 crisis pastoral care situations, this book provides a brief, practical guide for church leaders and other caregivers responding to stressful situations in the lives of parishioners. It tells how to resource caregiving professionals in the community who can help people in distress.

978-1-57312-370-9 154 pages/pb **$15.00**

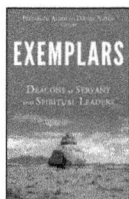

Exemplars
Deacons as Servant and Spiritual Leaders
Elizabeth Allen and Daniel Vestal, eds.

Who Do Deacons Need to Be? What Do Deacons Need to Know? What Do Deacons Need to Do? These three questions form the basis for *Exemplars: Deacons as Servant and Spiritual Leaders*. They are designed to encourage robust conversation within diaconates as well as between deacons, clergy, and other laity.   978-1-57312-876-6 128 pages/pb **$15.00**

The Exile and Beyond (All the Bible series)
Wayne Ballard

The Exile and Beyond brings to life the sacred literature of Israel and Judah that comprises the exilic and postexilic communities of faith. It covers Ezekiel, Isaiah, Haggai, Zechariah, Malachi, 1 & 2 Chronicles, Ezra, Nehemiah, Joel, Jonah, Song of Songs, Esther, and Daniel.   978-1-57312-759-2 196 pages/pb **$16.00**

Fierce Love
Desperate Measures for Desperate Times
Jeanie Miley

Fierce Love is about learning to see yourself and know yourself as a conduit of love, operating from a full heart instead of trying to find someone to whom you can hook up your emotional hose and fill up your empty heart.   978-1-57312-810-0 276 pages/pb **$18.00**

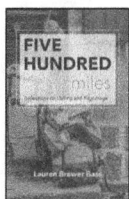

Five Hundred Miles
Reflections on Calling and Pilgrimage
Lauren Brewer Bass

Spain's Camino de Santiago, the Way of St. James, has been a cherished pilgrimage path for centuries, visited by countless people searching for healing, solace, purpose, and hope. These stories from her five-hundred-mile-walk is Lauren Brewer Bass's honest look at the often winding, always surprising journey of a calling.   978-1-57312-812-4 142 pages/pb **$16.00**

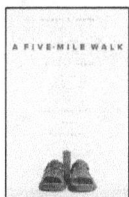

A Five-Mile Walk
Exploring Themes in the Experience of Christian Faith and Discipleship
Michael B. Brown

Sometimes the Christian journey is a stroll along quiet shores. Other times it is an uphill climb on narrow, snow-covered mountain paths. Usually, it is simply walking in the direction of wholeness, one step after another, sometimes even two steps forward and one step back.

978-1-57312-852-0 196 pages/pb **$18.00**

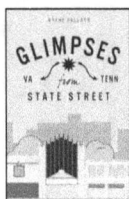

Glimpses from State Street
Wayne Ballard

As a collection of devotionals, *Glimpses from State Street* provides a wealth of insights and new ways to consider and develop our fellowship with Christ. It also serves as a window into the relationship between a small town pastor and a welcoming congregation.

978-1-57312-841-4 158 pages/pb **$15.00**

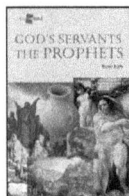

God's Servants, the Prophets
Bryan Bibb

God's Servants, the Prophets covers the Israelite and Judean prophetic literature from the preexilic period. It includes Amos, Hosea, Isaiah, Micah, Zephaniah, Nahum, Habakkuk, Jeremiah, and Obadiah.

978-1-57312-758-5 208 pages/pb **$16.00**

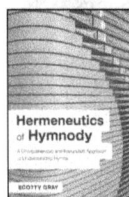

Hermeneutics of Hymnody
A Comprehensive and Integrated Approach to Understanding Hymns
Scotty Gray

Scotty Gray's *Hermeneutics of Hymnody* is a comprehensive and integrated approach to understanding hymns. It is unique in its holistic and interrelated exploration of seven of the broad facets of this most basic forms of Christian literature. A chapter is devoted to each and relates that facet to all of the others.

978-157312-767-7 432 pages/pb **$28.00**

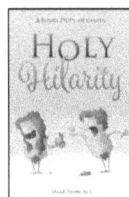

Holy Hilarity
A Funny Study of Genesis
Mark Roncace

In this fun, meaningful, and practical study of Genesis, Mark Roncace brings readers fifty-three short chapters of wit and amusing observations about the biblical stories, followed by five thought-provoking questions for individual reflection or group discussion. Humorous, yet reverent, this refreshing approach to Bible study invites us, whatever our background, to wrestle with the issues in the text and discover the ways those issues intersect our own messy lives. It's seriously entertaining.

978-157312-892-6 230 pages/pb **$17.00**

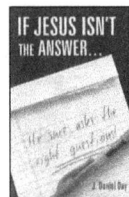

If Jesus Isn't the Answer . . . He Sure Asks the Right Questions!
J. Daniel Day

Taking eleven of Jesus' questions as its core, Day invites readers into their own conversation with Jesus. Equal parts testimony, theological instruction, pastoral counseling, and autobiography, the book is ultimately an invitation to honest Christian discipleship.

978-1-57312-797-4 148 pages/pb **$16.00**

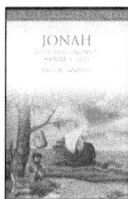

Jonah (Annual Bible Study series)
Reluctant Prophet, Merciful God
Taylor Sandlin

The book of Jonah invites readers to ask important questions about who God is and who God calls us to be in response. Along with the prophet, we ask questions such as What kind of God is the God of Israel? and Who falls within the sphere of God's care? Most importantly, perhaps, we find ourselves asking How will I respond when I discover that God loves the people I love to hate? These sessions invite readers to wrestle with these questions and others like them as we discover God's mercy for both the worst of sinners and the most reluctant of prophets.
Teaching Guide 978-1-57312-910-7 164 pages/pb **$14.00**
Study Guide 978-1-57312-911-4 96 pages/pb **$6.00**

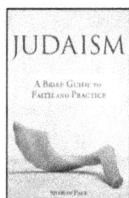

Judaism
A Brief Guide to Faith and Practice
Sharon Pace

Sharon Pace's newest book is a sensitive and comprehensive introduction to Judaism. How does belief in the One God and a universal morality shape the way in which Jews see the world? How does one find meaning in life and the courage to endure suffering? How does one mark joy and forge community ties?
978-1-57312-644-1 144 pages/pb **$16.00**

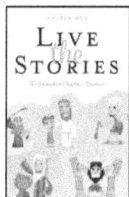

Live the Stories
50 Interactive Children's Sermons
Andrew Noe

Live the Stories provides church leaders a practical guide to teaching children during the worship service through play—and invites the rest of the congregation to join the fun. Noe's lessons allow children to play, laugh, and act out the stories of our faith and turn the sanctuary into a living testimony to what God has done in the past, is doing in the present, and will do in the future. As they learn the stories and grow, our children will develop in their faith.
978-1-57312-943-5 128 pages/pb **$14.00**

Loyal Dissenters
Reading Scripture and Talking Freedom with 17th-century English Baptists
Lee Canipe

When Baptists in 17th-century England wanted to talk about freedom, they unfailingly began by reading the Bible—and what they found in Scripture inspired their compelling (and, ultimately, successful) arguments for religious liberty. In an age of widespread anxiety, suspicion, and hostility, these early Baptists refused to worship God in keeping with the king's command.
978-1-57312-872-8 178 pages/pb **$19.00**

Meditations on Luke
Daily Devotions from the Gentile Physician
Chris Cadenhead

Readers searching for a fresh encounter with Scripture can delve into *Meditations on Luke*, a collection of daily devotions intended to guide the reader through the book of Luke, which gives us some of the most memorable stories in all of Scripture. The Scripture, response, and prayer will guide readers' own meditations as they listen and respond to God's voice, coming to us through Luke's Gospel. 978-1-57312-947-3 328 pages/pb **$22.00**

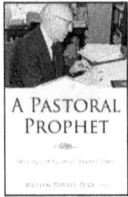

A Pastoral Prophet
Sermons and Prayers of Wayne E. Oates
William Powell Tuck, ed.

Read these sermons and prayers and look directly into the heart of Wayne Oates. He was a consummate counselor, theologian, and writer, but first of all he was a pastor. . . . He gave voice to our deepest hurts, then followed with words we long to hear: you are not alone.

—Kay Shurden
Associate Professor Emeritus, Clinical Education,
Mercer University School of Medicine, Macon, Georgia
978-157312-955-8 160 pages/pb **$18.00**

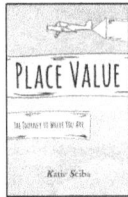

Place Value
The Journey to Where You Are
Katie Sciba

Does a place have value? Can a place change us? Is it possible for God to use the place you are in to form you? From Victoria, Texas to Indonesia, Belize, Australia, and beyond, Katie Sciba's wanderlust serves as a framework to understand your own places of deep emotion and how God may have been weaving redemption around you all along.
978-157312-829-2 138 pages/pb **$15.00**

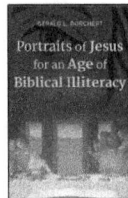

Portraits of Jesus
for an Age of Biblical Illiteracy
Gerald L. Borchert

Despite our era of communication and information overload, biblical illiteracy is widespread. In *Portraits of Jesus*, Gerald L. Borchert assists both ministers and laypeople with a return to what the New Testament writers say about this stunning Jesus who shocked the world and called a small company of believers into an electrifying transformation.
978-157312-940-4 212 pages/pb **$20.00**

Preaching that Connects
Charles B. Bugg and Alan Redditt

How does the minister stay focused on the holy when the daily demands of the church seem relentless? How do we come to a preaching event with a sense that God is working in us and through us? In *Preaching that Connects*, Charles Bugg and Alan Redditt explore the balancing act of a minister's authority as preacher, sharing what the congregation needs to hear, and the communal role as pastor, listening to God alongside congregants.   978-157312-887-2 128 pages/pb **$15.00**

Reading Isaiah
(Reading the Old Testament series)
A Literary and Theological Commentary
Hyun Chul Paul Kim

While closely exegeting key issues of each chapter, this commentary also explores interpretive relevance and significance between ancient texts and the modern world. Engaging with theological messages of the book of Isaiah as a unified whole, the commentary will both illuminate and inspire readers to wrestle with its theological implications for today's church and society.

978-1-57312-925-1 352 pages/pb **$33.00**

Reading Jeremiah
(Reading the Old Testament series)
A Literary and Theological Commentary
Corrine Carvalho

Reflecting the ways that communal tragedy permeates communal identity, the book of Jeremiah as literary text embodies the confusion, disorientation, and search for meaning that all such tragedy elicits. Just as the fall of Jerusalem fractured the Judean community and undercut every foundation on which it built its identity, so too the book itself (or more properly, the scroll) jumbles images, genres, and perspectives.   978-1-57312-924-4 186 pages/pb **$32.00**

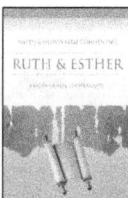

Ruth & Esther (Smyth & Helwys Bible Commentary)
Kandy Queen-Sutherland

Ruth and Esther are the only two women for whom books of the Hebrew Bible are named. This distinction in itself sets the books apart from other biblical texts that bear male names, address the community through its male members, recall the workings of God and human history through a predominately male perspective, and look to the future through male heirs. These books are particularly stories of survival. The story of Ruth focuses on the survival of a family; Esther focuses on the survival of a people.   978-1-57312-891-9 544 pages/hc **$60.00**

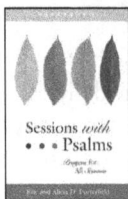

Sessions with Psalms (Sessions Bible Studies series)
Prayers for All Seasons
Eric and Alicia D. Porterfield

Useful to seminar leaders during preparation and group discussion, as well as in individual Bible study, *Sessions with Psalms* is a ten-session study designed to explore what it looks like for the words of the psalms to become the words of our prayers. Each session is followed by a thought-provoking page of questions. 978-1-57312-768-4 *136 pages/pb* **$14.00**

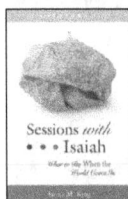

Sessions with Isaiah (Sessions Bible Studies series)
What to Do When the World Caves In
James M. King

The book of Isaiah begins in the years of national stress when, under various kings, Israel was surrounded by more powerful neighbors and foolishly sought foreign alliances rather than dependence on Yahweh. It continues with the natural result of that unfaithfulness: conquest by the great power in the region, Babylon, and the captivity of many of Israel's best and brightest in that foreign land. The book concludes anticipating their return to the land of promise and strong admonitions about the people's conduct—but we also hear God's reassuring messages of comfort and restoration, offered to all who repent. 978-1-57312-942-8 *130 pages/pb* **$14.00**

Stained-Glass Millennials
Rob Lee

We've heard the narrative that millennials are done with the institutional church; they've packed up and left. This book is an alternative to that story and chronicles the journey of millennials who are investing their lives in the institution because they believe in the church's resurrecting power. Through anecdotes and interviews, Rob Lee takes readers on a journey toward God's unfolding future for the church, a beloved institution in desperate need of change. 978-1-57312-926-8 *156 pages/pb* **$16.00**

Star Thrower
A Pastor's Handbook
William Powell Tuck

In *Star Thrower: A Pastor's Handbook*, William Powell Tuck draws on over fifty years of experience to share his perspective on being an effective pastor. He describes techniques for sermon preparation, pastoral care, and church administration, as well as for conducting Communion, funeral, wedding, and baptismal services. He also includes advice for working with laity and church staff, coping with church conflict, and nurturing one's own spiritual and family life. 978-1-57312-889-6 *244 pages/pb* **$15.00**

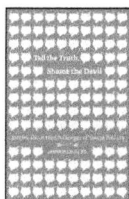

Tell the Truth, Shame the Devil
Stories about the Challenges of Young Pastors
James Elllis III, ed.

A pastor's life is uniquely difficult. *Tell the Truth, Shame the Devil*, then, is an attempt to expose some of the challenges that young clergy often face. While not exhaustive, this collection of essays is a superbly compelling and diverse introduction to how tough being a pastor under the age of thirty-five can be.　　　978-1-57312-839-1　198 pages/pb　**$18.00**

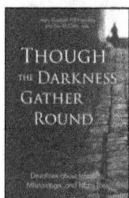

Though the Darkness Gather Round
Devotions about Infertility, Miscarriage, and Infant Loss
Mary Elizabeth Hill Hanchey and Erin McClain, eds.

Much courage is required to weather the long grief of infertility and the sudden grief of miscarriage and infant loss. This collection of devotions by men and women, ministers, chaplains, and lay leaders who can speak of such sorrow, is a much-needed resource and precious gift for families on this journey and the faith communities that walk beside them.

978-1-57312-811-7　180 pages/pb　**$19.00**

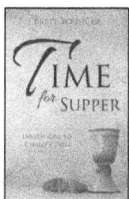

Time for Supper
Invitations to Christ's Table
Brett Younger

Some scholars suggest that every meal in literature is a communion scene. Could every meal in the Bible be a communion text? Could every passage be an invitation to God's grace? These meditations on the Lord's Supper help us listen to the myriad of ways God invites us to gratefully, reverently, and joyfully share the cup of Christ.　　978-1-57312-720-2　246 pages/pb　**$18.00**

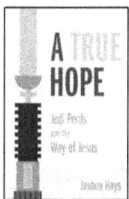

A True Hope
Jedi Perils and the Way of Jesus
Joshua Hays

Star Wars offers an accessible starting point for considering substantive issues of faith, philosophy, and ethics. In *A True Hope*, Joshua Hays explores some of these challenging ideas through the sayings of the Jedi Masters, examining the ways the worldview of the Jedi is at odds with that of the Bible.　　　978-1-57312-770-7　186 pages/pb　**$18.00**

www.ingramcontent.com/pod-product-compliance
Lightning Source LLC
Chambersburg PA
CBHW052133270326
41930CB00012B/2861